How Rob Ford Happened

How Rob Ford Happened

A History of the Toronto Mayor from the Pages of the *National Post*

HarperCollins*PublishersLtd*

Published by HarperCollins Publishers Ltd

First edition

The columns reproduced in this book have all previously appeared
in print and/or online editions of the *National Post*.

HarperCollins books may be purchased for educational, business,
or sales promotional use through our Special Markets Department.

HarperCollins Publishers Ltd
2 Bloor Street East, 20th Floor
Toronto, Ontario, Canada
M4W 1A8

www.harpercollins.ca

Library and Archives Canada Cataloguing in Publication
information is available upon request

ISBN 978-1-44343-588-8

Printed and bound in Canada
TC 9 8 7 6 5 4 3 2 1

Contents

How Rob Ford Happened

CHAMPION

FOR THE

LITTLE GUY

Ford is known for his outbursts

Fri Feb 28 2003

By: James Cowan

Since he was elected in 2000, Rob Ford has become known for his frequent and volatile outbursts in the Toronto council chamber. In the past year alone, he is alleged to have called another councillor a "Gino Boy," accused a city staff member of "skullduggery" and raged against "the left-wing nut jobs" on city council. Here is a chronology of the councillor's low points from the past year:

MARCH 6, 2002: Mr. Ford begins his feud with Councillor George Mammoliti, calling Mr. Mammoliti a "tough guy" and a "scammer," prompting the councillor to call Mr. Ford a "goon." Two days of attacks climax when Mr. Ford allegedly refers to Mr. Mammoliti as a "Gino boy." He denies using the racial slur, despite

Maria Augimeri, a nearby councillor, corroborating Mr. Mammoliti's claims.

Nov. 28, 2002: The councillor asks why a $100,000 contract for a children's water park has been given to the construction company of P. Gabriel and Sons. When staff state that Molson's, which donated the money for the park, selected the company, Mr. Ford challenges their assertion.

"You know what? I'm not going to get down and dirty, but the people who run this city told me right to my face that Molson's chose. So I just get off the phone from Molson's, and they're swearing up and down on a stack of Bibles that they did not choose this company. Well then, who chose P. Gabriel and Sons to build this water park for $100,000? Who?" he bellows.

Joe Halstead, the commissioner of Economic Development, Culture and Tourism, attempts to explain the situation to Mr. Ford.

"I told you what I know of it, my staff told me that it was Molson's," said Mr. Halstead.

"But you just talked to Molson's. And they said they didn't," interjects Mr. Ford, who proceeds to complain of "skullduggery."

A motion is put forward to eject Mr. Ford from the council chambers, but he withdraws his accusation instead.

FEB. 25, 2003: Councillor Howard Moscoe suggests an audit of police overtime.

"I'm going to try and remain calm," begins Mr. Ford's response to the motion, "but it just makes me sick when you left-wing nut jobs like Howard Moscoe are down here trying to bash the police non-stop. I feel embarrassed for [Chief Julian Fantino] to come here. If he wants to go after overtime, why doesn't he go after his own people's overtime and all their wasted money. Why don't you go after everyone, Mr. Moscoe? No, you don't because you're a police basher, your whole left-wing contingent down here, you're just a bunch of left-wing socialists that just attack and attack the police. You criticize and tell them they're racist, you tell them everything. Well, I've got news for you, you should travel around the world and see how fortunate we are to have a strong police force. . . . It just burns me up you can sit here and. . . . People are young. They're aggressive men and women of the police force, they want to get ahead in life. Maybe you don't, but when I was young, I wanted to go out and work 50, 60 hours and support my family. Not attack people for working overtime. That's embarrassing. That's a sickness to have someone like you making these motions. I will not support it."

Councillor's sister shot in home invasion: Suspects steal Jaguar

FRI APR 1 2005
By: Michael Friscolanti and Nicholas Kohler

The sister of outspoken Toronto City Councillor Rob Ford was shot in the face as she stood in her kitchen yesterday—a bold daylight attack that ended with two suspects fleeing the scene in the family Jaguar.

Investigators are hunting two suspects believed to have fled the Etobicoke home of Kathy Ford after she was shot shortly after 4 p.m. The 45-year-old woman was transported to Sunnybrook Hospital in serious condition.

Police Superintendent Ron Traverner confirmed she is the sister of Mr. Ford, the flamboyant representative for Ward 2 Etobicoke North, and the daughter of former Ontario Progressive Conservative MPP Doug Ford, who served one term in Mike Harris's provincial government.

Police said Ms. Ford was shot in the face by two men who yesterday stormed her home on Weston Wood Road, in the Royal York Drive and Eglinton Avenue area.

In a dramatic turn of events, Emergency Medical Services personnel and her children witnessed the two suspects fleeing the scene in the late-model black four-door Jaguar police say the suspects stole from the home, where Ms. Ford and her two children live with Ms. Ford's parents.

Police last night were attempting to contact Doug and Diane Ford, who are travelling in Florida.

Councillor Ford was seen yesterday at the scene, where he remained until police escorted him away for an interview.

Supt. Traverner called the woman's injuries "non-life threatening," adding that she was drifting in and out of consciousness in the aftermath of her ordeal.

The woman was spending yesterday at the home with a female friend and her two children—a 17-year-old daughter and an 11-year-old son—when the attack began, Supt. Traverner said.

The shooting took place in the home's kitchen, though police would not say whether Ms. Ford's two children witnessed the event.

Police said there was no sign of a forced entry, but could not say whether a struggle preceded the shooting.

No weapons were recovered.

In addition, at the end of a cul-de-sac, the location of the home would present a tactical problem for suspects looking for a quick escape.

Supt. Traverner cooled but did not deny speculation that the shooting was the end result of a home invasion, adding, however: "I wouldn't say that it's random, no."

He agreed that the two suspects may have known someone present in the home yesterday.

"It's certainly a possibility," he said. "But it could have been a knock on the door. People open doors and that's why I don't want to speculate at this point."

Police are seeking the stolen black Jaguar, which is owned by someone in the Ford household other than Ms. Ford, and two men, whom they describe as "white" and "brown."

Surveillance cameras in the area may shed light on yesterday's events, police said.

Last night, Gaye Fisher, who said she was Ms. Ford's friend of 29 years, collapsed in tears outside the Weston Wood home after racing to the scene from near Orangeville.

"She's beautiful," she said. "She's one of the most caring people that I've ever known."

Neighbours say they know the family who has lived for years in the house at the end of Weston Wood Road as quiet and industrious.

"The Fords are very quiet people; I like them," Lena Welssert, 69, told the *National Post* yesterday.

Those who follow Toronto city politics know Ms. Ford's brother, Rob Ford, for something other than his silence. Since his election in 2000, Mr. Ford has developed a reputation as a city councillor with a deep commitment to police issues.

Two years ago, when Councillor Howard Moscoe suggested an audit of police overtime, Councillor Ford struggled to retain his composure.

"It just makes me sick when you left-wing nut jobs like Howard Moscoe are down here trying to bash the police non-stop," he said at the time. "I feel embarrassed for [then Chief Julian Fantino] to come here."

Drug link to Ford shooting: History of gun violence: Husband gunned down child's father seven years ago

SAT APR 2 2005
By: Michael Friscolanti and Nicholas Kohler

Toronto police are treating the shooting of a city councillor's sister as a drug-related crime.

Detectives interviewed the 45-year-old victim, Kathy
Ford, at Toronto's Sunnybrook Hospital, where she is
coherent and recovering after a gunman fired a bullet
that grazed the top of her head.

Staff Sergeant Jack Kelly said yesterday the shooter
and his accomplice were invited inside for what appears
to be a drug deal gone awry.

"It has something to do with the purchase of drugs, a
disagreement regarding the purchase of drugs," he said,

refusing to elaborate on what role Ms. Ford might have played.

For those close to the family, Thursday's shooting dredged up memories of another crime involving Ms. Ford and her two children.

In July, 1998, the woman and her daughter—then 11—watched as a shotgun-wielding intruder opened fire on the young girl's father, Michael Kiklas.

The gunman was Ennio Stirpe, Ms. Ford's husband and the father of her then-infant son. Citing abuse, Ms. Ford had recently left Stirpe and gone to live with Mr. Kiklas, her high school sweetheart.

After fleeing the murder scene, Stirpe led police on a three-day manhunt that ended in a high-speed chase along Highway 401 in Durham Region. A cruiser pinned Stirpe's stolen station wagon against a guardrail.

When officers later escorted him from a hospital to his jail cell, he yelled to reporters: "See you in court, boys."

Journalists covered Stirpe's second-degree murder trial, but scant mention was made of Ms. Ford's link to the case, despite her family's prominent political background. Doug Ford, her father, was at the time an Ontario MPP in Mike Harris's Conservative government and her brother, Rob Ford, is a Toronto city councillor.

As a witness to the crime, she was a key Crown witness, describing how Mr. Kiklas, an avid kickboxer, tried to protect her and the two children moments before he was killed.

"It's sad," Rick Schwarzl, the Crown attorney who prosecuted the case, said of Thursday's shooting. "It is the second time in her life she has looked down the barrel of a gun. It's horrific."

In June, 2000, a judge found Stirpe guilty of manslaughter and sentenced him to 13 years in prison. He was also slapped with a $10,000 bill for Mr. Kiklas's funeral.

Tania MacDonald, Mr. Kiklas's sister, said she worries that her niece—now 17—will be overcome by the unenviable burden of having lived through the shootings of both her parents.

She and her 11-year-old brother were outside when their mother was shot in the kitchen, but they did watch the alleged gunman peel away in the family Jaguar. They called 911 moments later.

"She's gone through a lot in the last few years," Ms. MacDonald said of her niece. The *National Post* has decided not to print the names of Ms. Ford's children.

Ms. MacDonald planned to visit Ms. Ford in the hospital yesterday, but decided to wait for official confirmation that the shooting was not linked to the murder of her brother. During the trial, Stirpe repeatedly threatened her family, and even though he remains behind bars, she fears he is still dangerous.

"I'm a little concerned," she said. "I'm worried about my niece. I'm worried about Kathy. And I'd really like to know that it didn't have anything to do with Ennio Stirpe."

Police have not officially said so, but it appears they have ruled out that possibility. In fact, sources close to Councillor Ford say the family has been told Stirpe definitely had nothing to do with the shooting.

Acting on a tip, police pulled over the Fords' black Jaguar yesterday morning. The two men inside were questioned and charged with weapons-related offences and are being held until forensic investigators finish processing the crime scene.

Detectives are also questioning an unidentified woman who was in the house at the time of the shooting.

Staff Sgt. Kelly said investigators are still trying to figure out what type of drugs were involved, who was buying and who was selling.

In the meantime, the Ford family has asked for privacy, saying in a prepared statement that they appreciate "the outpouring of support from friends, councillor colleagues and the community at large."

Kathy Ford's parents, Doug and Diane, have owned the home where the shooting occurred for more than three decades. Rob and Kathy grew up there, and Kathy now lives there with her parents and two children.

Gaye Fisher, a close friend of Ms. Ford's, visited her in the hospital yesterday.

"She was in and out of consciousness," she said. "I said: 'Kathy, what's going on?' And she said: 'Gaye, I don't know what's going on. I don't know what's going on.' That is all she kept saying."

"She's been through enough and I hope this is it for her," she continued. "Her whole life has just been one traumatic thing after another. For some people, that's just the way things work."

Help will kill addicts: Ford

Tue Oct 18 2005
By: James Cowan

Toronto should consider building crematoria beside crack houses if the city's proposed drug strategy is implemented, City Councillor Rob Ford warned yesterday.

The councillor, who has battled addiction in his own family, blasted a new report by Toronto Public Health on combating alcohol and drug use in the city. The report recommends the city distribute crack pipes and other paraphernalia to addicts and explore opening safe injection and inhalation sites.

"It's euthanasia. You're just giving them a place to kill themselves. That's what is going to happen. You might as well just have a crematorium beside the crack house," Mr. Ford said.

He said these "harm reduction" strategies only encourage addicts to continue their drug use.

"You're not helping them, you're enabling them," Mr. Ford said. "They're going to smoke that crack whether you give them those crack pipes or not. They're going to shoot that heroin whether you give them clean needles or not. If people want a change, it has to come from within."

Mr. Ford has vocally opposed the city's support of harm-reduction strategies in the past, including a program at the Seaton House shelter that distributes wine and cigarettes to addicts.

According to the drug strategy, such harm-reduction measures as "safer crack use kits" may prevent the spread of disease between users. In addition, they allow outreach workers to connect with addicts and build trust.

The strategy also calls for better public education, increased treatment programs and a 24-hour crisis centre to help addicts.

Mr. Ford said the city should concentrate on enforcement and rehabilitation measures.

"You have to get these people into rehabilitation, and if they don't want to go, well, then you just enforce the law. If it's illegal, you arrest them. That's the bottom line, and if they have to dry out in jail—great," he said.

Mr. Ford said problems in his own family have taught him "tough love" is the only way to battle drug use.

The councillor's sister was shot and wounded this past March during an altercation in her parents' home. One of the men involved in the shooting was charged with cocaine possession.

"I know for a fact that tough love has worked, and I'm talking from personal experience. If you just enable someone and give them a place to live and money, nothing changes," Mr. Ford said.

"Safe" crack kits to fight addiction: Council approves controversial measures

THU DEC 15 2005
By: James Cowan

Toronto city council yesterday endorsed a new strategy to combat drug addiction, narrowly approving controversial measures such as providing crack pipes to addicts and further study of safe injection sites.

The plan proposed by Toronto Public Health contains 66 recommendations, including the creation of a 24-hour crisis centre for addicts and restricting the number of liquor licences in a single neighbourhood.

Only a handful of the proposals drew controversy. Councillors came within one vote of removing a provision calling for expanded harm reduction strategies, including the distribution of "safe" crack kits.

A recommendation supporting the decriminaliza-

tion of marijuana also survived, as did the recommendation calling for the city to study opening a safe injection
site, similar to one operating in Vancouver.

Councillor Kyle Rae, who championed the report,
said he was amazed the report passed in its entirety.

"I'm surprised that it got through," Mr. Rae said.
"But once in a while, there's a little twinge of leadership."

Among the other proposals are increased drug
enforcement efforts in public housing and a monitoring
system in hospitals and morgues for indications of new
street drugs in Toronto.

Opponents argued the plan will attract substance
abusers to Toronto. Councillor Rob Ford, who has battled addiction within his own family, said the strategy
will only help addicts harm themselves.

"Let me give you a suggestion on how you deal
with hard-core drug addicts," Mr. Ford said. "This is
not drinking wine or smoking a joint, this is heroin or
cocaine. With heroin or cocaine, you end up one of two
ways: dead or in jail. That's it. There's only two ways."

The councillor argued safe injection sites will
increase crime in the neighbourhoods surrounding
them.

"They're going to attract dealers; dealers are going
to carry guns. They're going to have prostitutes. It's the
worst scene you can possibly see. We're not helping anyone," Mr. Ford said.

A half-dozen members of Citizens for a Better

Toronto, a group opposed to the drug strategy, watched yesterday's debate in the council chamber. Linda Dixon said the proposal is too focused on helping drug users and not focused enough on protecting communities. "It's always about the drug dealer, it's never about us," Ms. Dixon said. "We're the ones who have to walk the streets, we're the ones who have to face these crackheads and dealers all the time. But we don't count."

Mayor David Miller disputed suggestions that the strategy would hurt neighbourhoods.

"It's not that by doing this, you make neighbourhoods weaker. By doing this, you make people stronger, so make neighbourhoods stronger," Mr. Miller said.

Supporters of the strategy said investing strictly in enforcement programs has failed to reduce drug use in the city. Councillor Shelley Carroll argued that rather than relying on police to eliminate drug use, the city should help drug users in order to eliminate other problems facing police.

"You have a gun problem, you have a violence problem and you have a crack problem, and if you don't recognize the connection between those three things, you are a doomed city," Ms. Carroll said.

Councillor Adam Giambrone noted enforcement is part of the overall drug strategy.

"I don't think there is anyone here who is saying we shouldn't be working with our police forces, we shouldn't be looking to deal with the drug dealers. . . .

Certainly we need to have those enforcement mecha-
nisms in place. But what we're doing here is recogniz-
ing a reality," he said.

Ford admits lying about Leafs game altercation: "I was inebriated"

WED MAY 3 2006
By: James Cowan

City Councillor Rob Ford yesterday admitted lying to reporters about causing a drunken fracas at a hockey game last month.

Mr. Ford initially denied attending a Maple Leafs game on April 15 at the Air Canada Centre, where he reportedly shouted insults at other fans.

But the councillor confessed yesterday that he had, in fact, attended the game.

"I had one too many beers and I sincerely apologize," he said. "I'm only human, and I made a mistake. I don't know what else I can say."

Mr. Ford also admitted he misled newspaper reporters when the allegations first arose.

When asked why he had denied attending the game, Mr. Ford said he "felt embarrassed."

During an interview with the *National Post* three days after the incident, the councillor claimed he had not attended a Leafs game since December.

"It's hard to be thrown out of [a] hockey game when you weren't even there," Mr. Ford told the *Post* at the time.

Mr. Ford said yesterday he did not believe lying to the media would damage his credibility.

"I'm honest," he said. "When I say I did it, I did it. I think that's as straightforward and honest as you can be. So we'll see what happens at election time. What else can I do? I work hard, it was in my own private time and when you're a politician, you are in the spotlight, and I made a mistake and I am deeply sorry for what I did. I've apologized and I will move on to doing my job as I've always done for the past six years."

Mr. Ford admitted he had behaved poorly after two fans, Dan and Rebecca Hope, filed a complaint with the city.

Their letter has been sent to David Mullan, the Integrity Commissioner, to determine whether an investigation is necessary.

The Integrity Commissioner does not have the jurisdiction to investigate the incident, according to Mr. Ford.

"This has nothing to do with City Hall; this has nothing to do with my job. It was my own private time. It was my own private tickets," Mr. Ford said.

Mr. Mullan declined to comment on whether he believed the incident fell within his mandate.

"Given that is going to be a contentious issue in this matter, I'm not going to make a comment one way or another," he said.

Mayor David Miller said it was "appropriate" that Mr. Ford had apologized for his behaviour.

"I think it was important for him to acknowledge what he had done and to apologize," Mr. Miller said. "As an elected official, I take my position very seriously, and I'm sure he's the same. It's important to acknowledge when you've done wrong."

Mr. Ford said he attended the hockey game and sat behind the visiting team's net along with his wife, Renata. Eyewitness accounts suggest Mr. Ford became engaged in a boisterous argument with other patrons, cursing heavily and referring to them as "communists."

But speaking with reporters yesterday, Mr. Ford denied making the remarks.

"I don't recall saying that, but I was inebriated, there's no doubt about it," he said.

The councillor said he was uncertain how much alcohol he consumed.

"I have no idea, but it was a lot, I had too many obviously," he said, adding, "I'm not a big drinker at all, so when I drink, it hits me pretty hard. I made a mistake. Maybe I shouldn't have drank at all. That's alcohol—it's a bad drug."

Mr. Ford denied the arena's security guards escorted him from the building.

"I think I left of my own free will," he said, adding, "I have nothing to say. It's water under the bridge. I feel embarrassed. I feel shameful. I don't know what more I can say. I made a huge mistake."

The "calm" Ford takes on all comers: Etobicoke incumbent rejects criticism he's more sound than fury

WED NOV 1 2006

By: Peter Kuitenbrouwer

If you think Councillor Rob Ford is loud, you should meet his big brother Doug. We are in the boardroom at Deco Labels & Tags, the family's printing business along Highway 401 in north Etobicoke, and Doug Ford is explaining Rob Ford's legendary outbursts on the floor of Toronto City Council.

"Sometimes the emotions get going and he sees councillors as pigs at the trough, ripping off the taxpayers," bellows Doug Ford. "If someone thinks they can do a better job than the Ford family and our 50 years of working for the community in north Etobicoke, then bring it on!"

Rob Ford leans back and smiles.

"I'm the calm one," he says.

Rob Ford is the youngest of four children of Doug and Diane Ford. Doug Ford, Sr., founded a printing business in his basement; the family-owned company now employs 100 at its Toronto plant and 50 at its plant in Chicago.

Doug Ford, Sr., served under Mike Harris as an MPP from 1995–99. (The father died last month, as his son tells me through tears.)

Rob Ford first won election to council in 2000, and is re-offering for the Nov. 13 vote.

I have always had a weak spot for the guy, who spends $4 of his $50,000 office budget, and who grills city staff without mercy during budget debates. But the Ford aura lost some of its lustre this spring, when Mr. Ford lied to reporters, including the *Post*'s James Cowan, when asked if he was drunk and disorderly at an April 15 Maple Leafs game.

"It's hard to be thrown out of a hockey game when you weren't even there," Mr. Ford told the *Post* on April 18. Then on May 2, he admitted that he was at the game, got drunk and caused trouble.

My grilling on this topic leads to another outburst by the older brother.

"Come on, he was drunk, he lied to the media, the next morning he went on the air and admitted it," Doug Ford says. "Move on. They're beating a dead horse."

Doug Ford then adds that, while he was canvassing on Sunday for his brother, an 85-year-old poet named Josephine Voltan came to the door and gave him a poem about Rob. Here are excerpts:

> He never fails to return a call;
> "Not so" of many at City Hall.
> So to all of you holier than thou,
> Watch Rob Ford take a bow;
> Really, why all this fuss;
> For a few beers and a little cuss.
> There are so many problems that need attention:
> Clean air, poverty and others too many to mention.
> So I say, "Cheers" to what he does best;
> And for God's sake, forget the rest.

Perhaps a less-sanctimonious councillor would have fared better in a similar affair. But let's give Mr. Ford his due: He does work hard for his constituents.

He pulls out a crumpled sheet of paper with his appointments. He visited five constituents before lunch yesterday: two women in social housing, one with a plugged toilet, another with a broken dryer; a homeowner whose neighbour's backyard was a mess; a man whose tree was overdue for a trim; and a man with water pooling in front of his house.

At each stop, he says, he brought staff. "I give city staff a week to get it done. If it is not done, I'll call Shirley Hoy, CEO of the city, and let her know staff is not doing their job."

But others think Mr. Ford is the one not doing his job.

After leaving the printing plant, I head to lunch with Mike McKenna, 24, at Danny D's on Attwell Drive, a friendly kind of working-man's bar next to the Metro West Detention Centre.

"We have the perception of being a rundown, low-income area, but that's not true," says Mr. McKenna, who lives in the basement of his parents' home in the ward and who has taken a leave from his job in the banking office at the Air Canada Centre to run for city council.

Mr. Ford not only lives outside the ward, but his behaviour at council is a big problem, Mr. McKenna says.

"When you break through all the yelling and screaming and ranting and raving, he doesn't get anything accomplished," says Mr. McKenna.

"I am going to bring an intelligent and respectful approach where we can work together and accomplish things."

Another candidate, Cadigia Ali, is a civil servant on leave from the Ministry of Community and Social Services. She wants to help the area's large Somali community.

"This area needs someone who can build a bridge to the mainstream so we can work together," she says.

That said, fighting the Ford family is a tough job. Mr. Ford prints his own signs, and yesterday his brother Randy's Ford truck was crammed to the grill with them. Diane Ford, the councillor's mother, also sported a Rob Ford sticker on her lapel and promised to make her boy a veal parmesan before an all-candidates' debate next week.

"Things are just great," Mr. Ford says. "I can't wait for Nov. 13."

Locals chase councillor out of neighbouring ward; "Go home, Rob Ford"

WED AUG 8 2007
By: Mark Medley

Councillor Rob Ford thought he was doing a good turn by showing up in a neighbouring ward to help people who were having headaches with road construction yesterday. But when he got there, Mr. Ford found instead an angry mob waving placards who chased him out of their community.

The Etobicoke politician went to the Humber-Sheppard Community Centre at 11 a.m. to meet with four residents who had called his office last week concerned about construction of a giant maple leaf made of interlocking brick at the intersection of Weston Road and Sheppard Avenue.

About 40 protesters were hiding in the hallway of the community centre. When Mr. Ford came walking along the sidewalk to enter the building, the group poured out and encircled him.

"Go home, Rob Ford!" they chanted, carrying cardboard signs with the slogans: "Get out of our ward, Rob Ford" and "Mind your own business, Rob Ford."

As Mr. Ford tried to talk to locals and reporters, jeers and chants drowned him out.

"It's none of his affairs," said Lou Santonato, the protest organizer who has lived in the area almost 40 years. "I didn't vote for the guy."

Mr. Ford said he supports the infrastructure work and was merely meeting with people who could not get answers from their own councillor, Giorgio Mammoliti. He called the protest "political grandstanding" on the part of Mr. Mammoliti.

"They didn't get an answer from their councillor, so I'm trying to help," Mr. Ford said.

Vivian Broersma, who showed up to meet Mr. Ford, said the protest was "a disgrace" and like "a mini-riot." She said that she was twice hit by signs and another woman was knocked to the ground. She had strong words for Mr. Mammoliti, who she believed orchestrated the protest.

"I have no use for the man whatsoever," she said. "He's just a pompous, arrogant, S.O.B. who has turned this ward into an absolute dictatorship."

The two councillors share a rocky past. In March, 2002, Mr. Ford called Mr. Mammoliti a "gino boy" and a "scammer."

In turn, Mr. Mammoliti called Mr. Ford a "goon." And in May, Mr. Mammoliti raised a motion at an executive committee meeting for Toronto's auditor-general and integrity commissioner to conduct an investigation into where Mr. Ford and Councillor Doug Holyday get the money to run their offices because they don't spend city resources.

Mr. Mammoliti was happy with the results of the protest.

"He went with his tail in-between his legs," he said. "I wish that every community he tries to move into, every ward that he tries to move into . . . would send him the same message."

Councillor unbowed over "Orientals" remark; Miller blasts Ford

FRI MAR 7 2008
By: Kelly Grant

Rob Ford, the city councillor best known for attacking his spendthrift colleagues, says he will gladly apologize to any Asian-Canadians hurt by his suggestion that industrious "Orientals" are "slowly taking over."

But Mr. Ford is refusing to say sorry on the council floor at the behest of Mayor David Miller—a rival the councillor says he is now "definitely considering" trying to unseat in the 2010 municipal election.

Mr. Ford made his controversial comments on Wednesday night during a council debate about extending holiday shopping to all downtown stores.

While urging council to go further and support city-wide openings 365 days a year, he said Torontonians should try working as hard as "Orientals."

"Go to the Orient. Go to Hong Kong. I've been there. You want to see workaholics? Those Oriental people work like dogs. They work their hearts out. . . . They sleep beside their machines. That's why they're successful in life," Mr. Ford said.

"Oriental people, they're slowly taking over. There's no excuses for [them]. They're hard, hard workers."

Mr. Miller, who was not in the chambers when Mr. Ford made his remarks, yesterday demanded he apologize.

"Councillor Ford's comments are totally inappropriate for anyone, let alone an elected official who represents a city that is probably the most diverse city in the world," the mayor said.

"Mr. Ford needs to make an apology; it needs to be made publicly on the floor of council and it should be to all Torontonians and to city council."

When told that Mr. Ford said he intended his speech as a compliment to the Asian community, Mr. Miller replied: "I don't think bigoted and racist comments can be meant as a compliment. I didn't know he'd said that. But I'm quite shocked that that would be the explanation."

Mr. Ford has developed a reputation for his off-the-cuff—and often off-colour—remarks.

In 2002, he called Giorgio Mammoliti, a councillor of Italian descent, a "Gino Boy," on the council floor. In 2006, he lied about getting drunk and hurling insults in the stands at a Toronto Maple Leafs game.

But the son of a former MPP also has plenty of devoted fans who appreciate his candid manner and careful attention to City Hall spending.

Yesterday, Mr. Ford showed off a stack of emails from supporters calling his Oriental speech harmless. Several of the messages entreated Mr. Ford to run for mayor.

"People have asked me, a ton of people have," said the Etobicoke councillor, who earlier mused about running for the top job before his inebriated turn at the Leafs' game in 2006.

"Now I'm definitely considering it."

If Mr. Ford does run, speeches such as the one he made this week could hurt his chances, some councillors said.

"Anybody could run for mayor, but as long as he makes this kind of remark, his chance of getting elected mayor is very slim," said Raymond Cho, a Scarborough councillor originally from Korea.

Others said the city should treat the remarks as a vintage Rob Ford media storm and ignore it.

"It was inappropriate," said Councillor Denzil Minnan-Wong, a critic of the mayor and a Chinese-Canadian. "I think city council has more important things to deal with than another Rob Ford outburst, and that we should just move on."

Mr. Ford said he would leave it to voters to judge his words.

"I don't respect the mayor. I never have. Hopefully he won't be our mayor in a couple of years. There's no secret about that. So if he wants to call me a racist or whatever, let the people decide. I'm not a racist."

Why this man is good for Toronto

Thu May 22 2008
By: David Menzies

Toronto City Councillor Rob Ford is very much like Don Cherry, the Pontiac Aztek and the anchovy as a pizza topping: you either loathe him or love him as there can be no murky middle ground. I unapologetically place myself in the latter camp.

No argument here that Ford can be abrasive. And perhaps he'd be wise to choose some of his words more carefully—if only for the purpose of denying his enemies the ammunition they so desperately crave for character assassination.

Yet, ironically, Ford's biggest bugaboo is also his most endearing quality: The successful businessman and high school football coach brings a common man's touch to an elitist political arena. Ford doesn't bother with three-dollar words, nor is he obsessed with the banalities of political correctness. Rather, like the major league umpire behind home plate, he calls 'em like he sees 'em. And in a political realm propelled by double-talk and BS, such honesty can be refreshing.

In the world according to Ford, there are three fundamental problems ailing the city, all of which impact upon the city's fiscal well-being.

For starters, Ford says the time has come to contract out city services, given that Toronto has become a fiefdom for powerful unions.

"The unions run the city because they run the mayor's office and the mayor is married to the unions," he says. "We [Toronto] could save hundreds of millions if we just contracted out some of our services. But the mayor won't even look at it."

Indeed, Ford notes that Toronto is the only municipality in Canada aside from Oshawa that has unionized garbage pickup. Contracting out garbage pickup alone would result in savings of approximately $20-million annually, he says.

The second debilitating problem is Toronto's bloated bureaucracy. By Ford's calculations, the city employs 7,000 more employees than what's actually needed to run the place. Worse, "the customer service stinks," he says. "Call City Hall and you get bounced around from department to department. We're paying people $50 an hour to do nothing."

Finally, Ford feels the TTC must be designated an

essential service. "They [transit workers] are holding our city hostage."

His opponents—and they are legion—bristle at the mere mention of Ford's name. And Ford's enemies can be a vindictive bunch. When it was revealed a while back that some city councillors were expensing items ranging from espresso machines to costume rentals, an investigation was launched. Alas, the investigation focused on Ford and fellow Etobicoke Councillor Doug Holyday, and why this duo was spending so few taxpayer dollars.

Meanwhile, for Torontonians older than 40, it's abundantly clear Toronto is no longer "New York run by the Swiss" as Peter Ustinov opined decades ago. Ford points to graffiti that's not removed; litter that's not picked up; grass that isn't cut; potholes that are ignored; aggressive panhandlers that are tolerated. . . . the list goes on. Ford makes certain to expose City Hall shenanigans and incompetence every Thursday morning on AM640's John Oakley Show, much to the delight of taxpayers and much to the chagrin of left-wing councillors.

In addition to his tireless whistle-blowing, Ford is now champing at the bit to take on Mayor David Miller. "I have one goal in mind and that is to become mayor," he says. "I'm a very optimistic person, and this city will run like a well-oiled machine when I'm mayor."

To paraphrase an old slogan from the automotive company: Will there be a Ford in Toronto's future? Let's hope so.

Why Rob Ford is bad for Toronto

Fri May 23 2008
By: John Moore

In yesterday's *Post*, writer David Menzies made the case in favour of bombastic Toronto Councillor Rob Ford, who plans to challenge Mayor David Miller in the next municipal election. Today, the case against.

The current low wattage in Toronto's civic administration makes any shiny thing seem like an attractive alternative, but when I hear that Rob Ford is contemplating a run at the mayoralty, I shudder. Ford's intentions are good, and he has a certain guileless charm that makes him welcome on my show any time, but he's not mayor material.

Outside of making a sloppy public spectacle of himself during a Leafs game and his now-resolved domestic contretemps, Ford's reputation consists largely of an ongoing cranky-pants attack on civic spending. Never one to sweat the big stuff, Ford mostly confines himself to the kind of petty cash shenanigans that irk more than enrage: $20,000 for cold sandwiches to tide peckish councillors over during long council sittings, councillors caught spending money on espresso machines and giant rabbit heads. But in a city with an $8-billion budget in 2008, this is like counting paperclips. True, it's the thought that counts, but one wishes Rob Ford had bigger thoughts.

In these pages yesterday, my friend David Menzies argued passionately that Ford is a man of the people who "calls 'em as he sees 'em," which prompts one to wonder precisely what Ford sees.

Ford's problems are legion. His propensity for malapropisms and politically incorrect utterances make former mayor Mel Lastman seem Churchillian in comparison. He has posited that women get HIV from philandering bisexuals and believes he is complimenting Asians when he says they are taking over. His solution for the city's homeless problem is that every drug-addled and mentally ill vagrant is a shower and finger-wagging lecture away from a job at the Gap.

While city councillors are supposed to be busy conceiving and executing a grand vision of Toronto's future, Ford occupies himself with piddling constituency concerns. A councillor who rushes to the scene of a water main burst and makes a grand show of supervising its repair will always appear to be on top of his game, but the real grunt work of administration is done in the dreary meeting rooms of City Hall.

If he runs for mayor, Ford will make union-bashing and privatization his mantra. This conveniently papers over the fact that about half of Toronto's services are already contracted out. Intriguingly, when Ford made a big fuss about cost overruns at the waterworks, it was revealed that one of the principal causes was overbilling by a private contractor.

Ford will rail against the greedy unions (excluding, no doubt, the police and firefighters, who always get a pass), because for right-wingers on council it's great to earn $95,000 a year arguing policy, but God forbid a worker operating heavy machinery or emptying trash bins be paid enough to buy a decent house and raise kids.

Ford comes from that school of economics where government is expected to cut taxes and provide more services. He and his unofficial caucus make much of how New York City solved its homeless problem without ever mentioning that it cost $10-billion.

Tellingly, the councillor's distaste for disbursements from the public purse evaporates when he's petitioning for his own ward. Only last year he interrupted his ongoing harangue about out-of-control spending to demand $750,000 worth of curbs and gutters for two streets in Etobicoke North.

Right-wingers are a rare breed at Toronto City Hall, which would explain why conservatives make heroes of the few there are, no matter how intemperate their character or minor their accomplishments. Rob Ford is like an approximation of a good conservative administrator. In a city that could use an injection of common sense and real-world management savvy, Ford is all nostrums and talking points and no action.

Scandal won't stop Ford, nor should it

FRI AUG 20 2010
By: Chris Selley

If drinking and driving couldn't bring down Gordon Campbell, and an addiction to "party drugs" couldn't bring down George Smitherman, drinking and driving with a joint in his pocket seems very unlikely to bring down Rob Ford.

On the record are his Ralph Klein-esque berating of homeless people, his Bobby Knight-esque coaching strategies, his drunken buffoonery at a Maple Leafs game, his impossibly juvenile squabbles with other councillors, his politically incorrect utterances about Asian-Canadians and people with AIDS . . . the list goes on.

The fact that he claimed not to have remembered being charged with marijuana possession because he was more concerned about being charged with failing to provide a breath sample—he was actually charged with, and pleaded guilty to, driving under the influence— might indeed turn out to be problematic.

Cumulatively, eventually, these foibles, and especially his talent for not owning up to them until absolutely necessary, are quite likely to keep him out of the mayor's office. But there's no reason to believe this will immediately impact his front-runner position in the mayoral race. While Mr. Campbell's good name was severely damaged, clearly the quality of Mr. Ford's name is largely beside the point—or he wouldn't be where he is in the polls in the first place.

It's obvious that much of Mr. Ford's popular support thus far exists as a protest against David Miller, his would-be successors and the political class in general. The city's Executive Committee opened a window into Mr. Ford's appeal this week when it expressed unanimous support for building the continent's tallest flagpole, which would fly the world's largest flag, at Finch Avenue and Highway 400.

This will be a tourist attraction—a tourist attraction . . . at Finch Avenue and Highway 400. (For the record, the world's tallest flagpole is currently in Jordan, soon to be usurped by flagpoles in Turkmenistan and Azerbaijan. That's our competition. It's like the Pan Am Games of roadside attractions.)

This won't cost us any money, ostensibly. It's to be funded by private business (though who knows how much it's already cost in staff and councillors' time?). But, arguably anyway, it's a fundamentally silly idea for politicians presiding over a city in financial crisis to even be talking about. One can just picture Mr. Ford railing against it—if only because it's the brainchild of Giorgio Mammoliti, his arch-nemesis on council—and one can picture people nodding in cynical agreement.

But Mr. Ford is tapping into something far less cynical, too—the aforementioned fiscal crisis. Also this week, the Executive Committee reinstated funding for Toronto's two piddling ski hills. (The city had put their operation out to private tender but, shockingly, there wasn't a single bid.) "Should we only allow skiing and snowboarding for rich kids?" Councillor Janet Davis asked rhetorically. "Absolutely not."

Replace "skiing and snowboarding" in that sentence with, say, "polo" or "hot-air ballooning," and she'd never have said it. But she's out to protect the status quo, even if over two years it's going to cost the city $600,000 that it just plain doesn't have. The municipal cupboard is bare, except for mountains of debt. Blame whomever you want. Mr. Ford is the one shouting it while his fellow candidates debate bike lanes and funding models for new subway construction that most Torontonians are quite sure will come to naught.

There's certainly an appeal to spite in Mr. Ford's promises to halt the gravy train, end the party, wrestle the pigs away from the trough. But there's also a burning need. The city's broke, and every $600,000 it spends makes it $600,000 broker. Someone has to wave his arms frantically about that situation, and for now that's Mr. Ford. Until Torontonians start asking themselves if a man who's been arrested so often he's forgotten some of them is capable of making the situation any better, his frontrunner status doesn't seem to be much in peril.

A backlash against the know-it-alls

TUE SEP 21 2010
By: Tasha Kheiriddin

On Wednesday, the House of Commons will decide the fate of the federal long-gun registry. If Candace Hoeppner's private member's bill dies, the registry will survive, and the debate will be over—for now. But the groundwork on the Conservatives' next election narrative will have just begun.

This standoff is about more than shotguns: It is laying bare political fault lines that have been obscured since the federal election of 2006. That's when Liberal communications director Scott Reid made his infamous quip about Canadian parents spending the Conservatives' proposed childcare allowance on "beer and popcorn" instead of on actual child care. Cue the populist revolt: Who knows better how to raise their children—state-funded daycares or mom and dad?

We're seeing the same dynamic at play now, with House Leader John Baird attacking the "Toronto elites" who support the gun registry. By those elites, it was assumed he was referring to Liberal leader Michael Ignatieff and NDP leader Jack Layton, currently engaged in so much whipping and arm-twisting, they risk arrest for MP abuse.

Mr. Baird's remark set off a predictable Tweet-storm, including a comment by Ontario's Minister of Research and Innovation, Glen Murray, accusing Mr. Baird of belonging to those selfsame elites. Observers asked: Why would the Conservatives want to alienate Toronto voters, when they could use more seats in urban Canada? (Of course, insulting Toronto always pays dividends in the rest of the country, which loves to hate Canada's largest city. It's like France hating Paris, minus the haute couture.)

The reality is, in suburban Toronto, the Tories could actually profit from this catfight. A large swath of the city apparently hates its elites as well, as evidenced by what is happening in the current race to replace outgoing Mayor David Miller. This week, a Nanos Research Poll put City Councillor Rob Ford in first place by a 24-point lead over his only real rival, former provincial Liberal health minister George Smitherman.

If ever there were a battle of elite vs. anti-elite, this is it. The downtown-based, openly-gay Mr. Smitherman has the blessing of the big- and small-L liberal establishment.

Meanwhile, the portly, plain-talking Mr. Ford questions the cost of integrating immigrants and rails against perks for elected officials. Critics and opponents deride him as a buffoon in a "cheap suit" who couldn't possibly represent a city as sophisticated and cosmopolitan as Toronto.

The irony, of course, is that Mr. Ford doesn't hail from Toronto's mean streets, or even its middle class. He is a successful businessman. His family owns one of the largest label-printing companies in the world. Mr. Ford foots his own council office expenses and gives generously to charity. Like patrician politicians of old, he clearly doesn't need the mayor's job to pay the bills.

But being an "elite" isn't about money; it's about mindset. It is about one's vision of the relationship between the citizen and the state: Should most decisions be made by a small, centralized group of those who "know best," or by the individual? On that question, Mr. Ford sympathizes with, and appeals to, the same "anti-elitists" (for lack of a better term) whom the federal Tories need to court in the next election, in Toronto and elsewhere.

While the reality is that governments can't function without elites (like it or not, elected officials have more power than you or me) they can function without elitism. This involves listening to both the wisdom of crowds and the "educated" opinions that interest groups and bureaucracies spout every day. These factions often are at odds on hot-button issues such as taxes, crime, illegal migrants, gun registries and childcare funding—as are the federal Conservative and Liberal parties.

So in the next national election, while the Tories' ballot question may be the economy, their narrative is likely to be that of the anti-elite party. Their opponents may have accused them of being "anti-knowledge" in the wake of the census debate, but Mr. Baird's comments turned that storyline on its head. The Tories aren't against smarts (Mr. Harper has plenty of those), they're against smugness.

Mr. Ford's lead shows they may be on to something: Apparently, people drink plenty of Tim Hortons in Toronto, too.

Political wisdom no match for Ford; Five myths trampled during improbable rise

Tue Sep 21 2010
By: Jonathan Kay

If polls are to be believed, the next mayor of Toronto is going to be Rob Ford—a man I had formerly always thought of (to the extent I thought of him at all) as the large, slightly hysterical city councillor (literally) chasing around *Globe and Mail* reporter John Barber in a heavily circulated 2008 YouTube video.

I won't presume to predict what kind of mayor Mr. Ford will be. But even before taking office, he has busted up at least five articles of received wisdom regarding Canadian politics.

Municipal politics is boring. Wrong: Ford shows us why the city beat actually can be more interesting. In the federal and provincial arenas, everyone is trying to protect their respective parties' brand, which is why they're so risk-averse and backwards-looking. Thus do federal Liberals endlessly navel-gaze about what "the party of Laurier" would do and their NDP counterparts slavishly hew to the union party line, as they've done for decades. On the provincial level here in Ontario, meanwhile, pundits and pols are still arguing 90s-era chestnuts about Mike Harris's common-sense revolution, and whether the current incarnation of the Tories should be held responsible for Walkerton and Ipperwash. Party-less free-agent loose cannons like Mr. Ford, on the other hand, don't have to carry around any of that baggage. Instead, they can mouth off about whatever they feel like—living and dying on the basis of their ideas instead of their brands.

The mass media—or even the new-fangled social media—shape voters' opinions. Wrong. For weeks now, the Toronto press has whipped itself into a frenzy about what sort of international laughingstock Toronto would become if this "buffoon" (Google that word alongside "Rob Ford" and you get almost 2,000 hits) were to become mayor. But no one cares. They don't even care about the Internet videos showing him freaking out, or those sophomoric Facebook groups with names like "Can this croissant get more fans than Councillor Rob Ford?"

All they seem to care about is their visceral conviction that Toronto has been wrecked by the sort of big-spending, union-coddling lefties against whom Mr. Ford rails.

The Canadian electorate is easily manipulated by spin doctors and political consultants. Wrong. A few weeks ago, Rocco Rossi went out and recruited a name-brand political consultant from the old Chretien-era Liberal machine, a man some people tout as a sort of Canadian Dick Morris. The result? Mr. Rossi, a Liberal insider hailed as a front-runner when he put his hat into the race—is now polling in single digits, fourth behind Mr. Ford, George Smitherman and Joe Pantalone. (So much for kicking ass in Canadian politics.)

People vote strategically. Wrong. For weeks, the *Toronto Star* has been making increasingly desperate and pathetic pleas for its readers to get behind George Smitherman as an anybody-but-Ford candidate. The editors even inserted this message into their front-page "news" story yesterday. But in recent weeks, the race really has been nothing more than the also-rans cannibalizing each other's vote share. Things could change by election day, but all signs point to a many-sliced vote-sharing pizza, with Mr. Ford eating a half all by himself.

Suburbanites are from Mars, urbanites are from Venus. Wrong. Whatever their differences over cars versus public transit, the pro-Ford phenomenon spans the GTA—something I didn't properly understand till I attended a Yom Kippur fast-breaking party on Saturday, in the elitist enclave of Forest Hill, a place I expected Ford to be a figure of mockery. "I'll be voting for him," said my cousin Danny. "I don't care how polished he is. He knows what's right."

As for me, I haven't decided whether I'll be voting for Mr. Ford or not. But I'll have a good chance to make up my mind when he comes in to the *National Post* for an editorial-board meeting this afternoon. We'll be serving croissants.

Rob Ford's charms may be his downfall

Wed Sep 22 2010
By: Chris Selley

Well, at least now we know where Rob Ford's going to get the $200-million or so he needs to axe the land-transfer and vehicle-registration taxes. It sure took some cajoling, though. Asked for the umpteenth time yesterday during a meeting with the *National Post* editorial board where these savings would be found, he for the umpteenth time railed against a famously sole-sourced subway car contract and a too-lavish refurbishment project for Nathan Phillips Square—money that, as has been pointed out umpteen times, has already been spent.

It's been less reminiscent of a mayoral candidate riding a rocket to City Hall than of an Abbott and Costello routine.

But Mr. Ford, apparently reluctantly, came clean yesterday: He'd get the money through attrition.

The city loses 6% of its workforce each year through attrition. Mr. Ford said he would replace only 3%. This is so downright plausible by comparison, it's tough to know why he sat on it for so long, looking all the while as if he didn't know the difference between the past and the future.

The 2010 budget allows more than $4-billion for salaries and benefits; 3% of that is somewhere about $120-million. Not all the way to Mr. Ford's tax cuts, but most of it. (He promises more details soon.) Combined with his now-famous nickel-and-dime cuts at City Hall—halving the number of councillors, slashing their expense accounts and staff complements—he might just be on to something.

How does Mr. Ford propose to cut the number of staff—not to mention the number of councillors and their staff—while ensuring City Hall provides vastly superior customer service, which is one of his bedrock (and understandably popular) pledges? That's tougher, conceptually. At least it is until you realize that the city's staff complement has grown 13% since 1998. Has customer service ameliorated over that time? Most Torontonians would likely say no. All voters susceptible to Mr. Ford's charms would likely say no.

Ultimately, though, those charms might be his downfall—if not during the campaign, which he is well-placed to win, then in the mayor's office. He's by no means unique in running a campaign full of promises that may or may not come to fruition. But he is unique in selling a campaign that's not just about fiscal conservatism but straight-up austerity. Asked yes or no on several planned projects, including further waterfront redevelopment, his answer was blunt: "We don't have the money." That's refreshing, and it's true. But is that what Torontonians really want, or do they just like the idea of kicking David Miller in the rear end?

What if Mr. Ford can't even deliver a livable austerity? You can't cut 3% of staff forever—at least not without affecting services.

More questions: Mr. Ford wants to divert $3.7-billion in provincial funding for Transit City streetcar projects to new subways: completing the Sheppard line and extending the Danforth line to meet it at Scarborough Town Centre. What makes him so confident the province—which has lopped off funding from Transit City itself, never mind subways—would play ball? "I'm pretty confident Mr. McGuinty will give me the money," said Mr. Ford. And if he doesn't? "I'll let Mr. McGuinty explain why we won't get subways." And how would that help, exactly?

I can almost see the potential backlash building. And that's just based on his policy follow-through. This is a man with some history. Asked if his arrests, verbal eruptions and unfortunate incidents were in his past, he claimed never to have found a perfect person and complained of living in a fish bowl. OK. Just like all those other councillors without criminal records, right?

"I can assure you Rob Ford would be a very well-respected mayor," he promised.

It's all he can do. But combine the "criticism and controversy" section of his Wikipedia page with a fiscal plan that's no more convincing than any other candidate's—I'm being charitable—and it's hard not to shudder at the stakes in this particular game of craps.

Ford and the real issues

Sat Oct 16 2010
By: Chris Selley

"There's nobody, but nobody, in politics that has helped out black people more than I have," quoth Rob Ford on Wednesday night during a mayoral debate at the Jamaican Canadian Centre, up Jane-and-Finch way. My jaw dropped slightly, and I checked to make sure my tape recorder was working. It was. He said it. Then I realized I seemed to be the most scandalized person in the room. Many people might assume Mr. Ford would be chased out of a debate like this, but he definitely wasn't.

Facing off against George Smitherman, Joe Pantalone and Rocco Achampong, I'd say he came close to winning it, and upon reflection it's not hard to see why.

The question Mr. Ford was answering—from a no-nonsense Jane and Finch resident named Cathy—went like this: "I want to know what you would do for us in this area, especially for our black men who are getting shot down in the street and no one is being held accountable for it. Also, I don't want to hear nothing about no basketball, no football, no soccer. We have bright, intelligent young people."

I laughed—not because it was funny, but the way you laugh when an idea you've always thought was reasonable is suddenly, convincingly denounced by someone with a totally different perspective: Of course not every young person at Jane and Finch wants to play sports, or is good enough at sports to make a team, let alone get a scholarship to university. Clearly, Coach Ford had no choice but to mention football—and he did—but I thought he carried it off reasonably well.

"A lot of time, kids don't want to go to school," he opined, uncontroversially. "So what we have to do is give them a carrot—something to convince them to go to school." His experience in football, he explained, was just one kind of carrot.

Unfortunately, the secondary schools in Ward 4, which includes Jane and Finch, remain among the very poorest performers in the TDSB, according to the Fraser Institute's rankings. And though we've heard amazingly little about issues of primary concern to the so-called "priority neighbourhoods"—poverty, the state of social housing, joblessness, education or lack thereof, violence—they haven't gone away.

There were fewer murders in Toronto last year than in any of the previous three years, but there weren't few; there were 62. There were more shootings than in any of the previous three years. In August, the three-month moving average unemployment rate in Toronto was 10.1%—nearly 25% above the national average.

You couldn't listen to the questions being asked on Wednesday night and miss the point. "It takes a healthy village to raise a child," one audience member observed, referring to the state of social housing. "My village is not healthy."

Mr. Pantalone's "everything's pretty much OK" message wasn't at all well-received.

The one person who has at least tried to bring these practical issues into the campaign limelight is Mr. Ford, said Mr. Achampong.

He speaks approvingly of Mr. Ford's standpoint on employment: "The best social program is a job," as Mr. Achampong puts it. "It's true."

One of the biggest cheers Mr. Ford got was when he said he'd hand rental subsidies directly to their recipients and let them live wherever they want, instead of leaving them to the mercies of Toronto Community Housing, which he always calls "the worst landlord in the city."

Mr. Achampong—whose tune seems to have changed considerably since August, when he called Mr. Ford "wrong-headed," "backward" and "not qualified to be mayor"—is similarly complimentary of Mr. Ford's football coaching career. "In academia, we sit around and have long conversations on causes and glorify each other to the point of near-deification. But who's doing something for people?" he asks. "They don't need published reports. They need results."

It's all good and proper that this campaign has been about City Hall's finances and the state of the TTC. These are critically important to the city as a whole, and no less to "priority neighbourhoods" like Jane and Finch. (I took the TTC to the debate from Yonge and Eglinton, just to remind myself how the neighbourhood fits into the city. Operating with unimpeachable efficiency, it took 75 minutes.)

But the Toronto-the-bad issues haven't gone away, and they aren't going away. It's not hard to believe Mr. Ford might be rather good at dealing with them. In any event, I think we might have been better off debating them instead of, say, bike lanes—which, by comparison, don't matter even a little bit.

THE MAYOR

OF

TORONTO

A right turn;
Penny-pinching Councillor Rob Ford rides populist wave to overwhelming victory in Toronto mayoral race; City has spoken, and it is angry

TUE OCT 26 2010
By: Chris Selley

One can only imagine the horror in certain quarters. Uncouth, uncultured, suburban, journalist-chasing, drunk driving, marijuana-possessing Air Canada Centre ejectee and lone wolf former city councillor Rob Ford is mayor-elect of Toronto—and not just by a little. Mayor David Miller congratulated him last night and so should everyone else. It sure won't help not to.

Whatever happens over the next four years, this election sent a hugely important message to Canadian politicians: Ignore voter anger at your peril. If you think voters shouldn't be angry, make your case early and sincerely. Don't just blame a senior level of government for your problems.

There is, of course, the matter of the next four years to consider. Mr. Ford says his first order of business today will be to call every single councillor and set up a meeting, and that could hardly be more important. He's got a city to run, and some good ideas. And the fact that he just successfully completed an incredibly even-tempered campaign suggests he may in fact be perfectly capable of building bridges, staffing committees with an eye toward progress and driving through some facsimile of his incredibly ambitious fiscal agenda—all the things we were haughtily assured he couldn't.

The fact remains: City Hall needs change in a bad way.

The "everything's OK" brigade was out in force in the final week of the campaign. "The city's finances are in good order," veteran NDP strategist Brian Topp declared in *The Globe and Mail*. In the *Toronto Star*, economist Hugh MacKenzie cracked wise about the balance book: "The city's finances are in such poor shape that the 2011 fiscal plan of every one of the candidates for mayor starts with a description of what they'd do with the surplus expected at the end of 2010."

Right. They'd all put the projected surplus against the $503-million budget shortfall facing the city in 2011 (more than that, once you add the cost of their campaign promises). That's the same kind of shortfall we face every year—the sort that rapidly precipitates TTC fare increases, property tax hikes, the introduction of car registration and land transfer taxes, chintzy across-the-board budget cuts and other frantic manoeuvres. To some extent, that's inevitable in a jurisdiction that can't legally run a deficit, but it's impossible to convince people things are under control in such a panic-based environment.

Anyway, the anger was more fundamental, and more thoughtful, than that. To tell people the budget is balanced, or that property taxes in Toronto are the lowest in the GTA, ignores the opportunity costs of wasteful spending.

There's no denying that the TTC—to pick the example most discussed during this campaign—is a dusty, hollow shell of what it could have been had more money been invested intelligently in public transit in recent years. Mr. Ford clearly doesn't understand transit, and it fills me with dread. But he says he can cut nearly $2-billion in the next four years through attrition and efficiencies alone, without impacting services. That's our money to use! Who in his right mind would object to him trying?

Mr. Ford should take solace and anti-Ford Torontonians and their councillors should take notice—that the mayor-elect has a tremendous mandate for change. Mr. Smitherman did not run a fiscally moderate platform, by Toronto standards. He promised big cuts of his own. And together, they won 83% of the vote. A subtle hint, it wasn't.

Councillors have their own mandates, of course, and no one should expect them to change their stripes completely. The mixed bag of results at the ward level doesn't suggest the great gravy train robbery trickled systematically down. (Though it's certainly tempting to see Sandra Bussin's ouster as a statement that certain behaviour just isn't acceptable anymore.) But nobody wants gridlock, and there are plenty of objectives on Mr. Ford's to-do list—notably open government initiatives— that could prove effective bridge-builders.

Opening up garbage collection to competitive bidding will be another interesting debate. This is not an "anti-union" measure. The replacement workers—if they were indeed replacements; CUPE could easily win the contract—would themselves almost certainly be unionized. But it would be a quick declaration that things are not as they were, that we've simply passed the point in history where something like trash pickup needs to be the exclusive domain of the public employee.

That will be an important test for the new council. If it freaks out, we'll know we're in trouble.

But if it passes, it would be a hugely important psychological step even if it didn't save a single dollar in 2011. I, for one, am optimistic.

Let the grand experiment begin!

ROB FORD (47%)
GEORGE SMITHERMAN (36%)
JOE PANTALONE (12%)

Crying into their frappuccinos

WED OCT 27 2010
By: Kelly McParland

Across Toronto yesterday morning bleary-eyed residents grabbed their two-wheelers and cycled to Starbucks, ordered up a stiff frappuccino—what the hell, make it 2% milk, I'll need it—and surveyed the damage.

It couldn't be true. Rob Ford, Mr. Double-Double, a guy who never met a cruller he didn't like, had pulled it off. The man got himself elected mayor. All those angry suburbanites, the ones who were supposed to complain a lot but skip the actual process of voting, had turned up en masse and put the guy in office.

For Toronto's urban sophisticates, it was a wipeout. Total repudiation. Worse than the time they ran out of well oaked chardonnay at Vintages. What are they supposed to do now, move to Calgary? Buy a leaf blower, for Christ sake? Any day now they'll be erecting barriers at Pusateri's, checking IDs. No one gets in without a credit card from Home Depot.

Wearily they munched their almond biscotti and totted up the devastation. Someone would have to contact the holistic, non-profit communal bike-sharing project and warn them the grand opening, scheduled for January, would be delayed.

Expansion of the rooftop lawn at City Hall would have to be put on ice, construction of the solar-powered arboretum delayed, shipments of biodegradable, non-toxic, soy-based weed control returned to the dealer. Oh, just keep the bloody deposit. Might as well just buy some mums at Costco and stick them in the lobby, like they do in Mississauga where that . . . woman . . . was re-elected once again. How old is she now, 300? She'll be more insufferable than ever, demanding we show up at some shopping mall and help coordinate bus routes. Hazel dear, we don't want your buses coordinating with ours, we want your people to stay home on weekends.

All across the city the scene at Starbucks was being repeated. The man in charge of closing the main access highways every weekend for kite-flying festivals and go-cart races was checking the want ads for job openings. Classes were cancelled at the new Streetcar Drivers' Training Centre, where they'd been practising how to arrive at stops in bunches of three or four at a time, 20 minutes behind schedule, without bumping into one another. There were nothing but sad faces at the Toronto Works yard, where they'd been busy digging up roads for seven years—the same ones, over and over—and now face the prospect of putting them all back together so people can actually drive on them.

David Miller's SUV driver, who knew to keep the motor running while the mayor made his annual Earth Day speech, was devastated. So were the taxi drivers outside TTC headquarters, who stand to lose all that business from commissioners taking cabs across town to discuss improving the transit system. Up in the planning department, where they'd been figuring out when to break the news of yet another fare hike so they could build themselves a new headquarters, gloom was everywhere. What's the point of working for the public transit system if you can't borrow money to build yourself a new office, conveniently near the highway and with plenty of free parking? Speaking of devastation, what about plans for the new four-storey hockey rink down near the waterfront, the one the old council wanted to build even though it would cost $88-million and it only had $34-million to pay for it? Don't even ask. You think Rob Ford's going to agree to borrow an extra $54-million for a rink where the Zambonis have to travel by elevator, just because it would be prettier than the alternative? Give up sweetheart. You ever see Rob Ford? You think he plays hockey?

Nope, it was just an ugly day all-round in poor old Toronto. The wailing was so loud it woke the ticket-takers on the Bloor subway line. Food inspectors, accustomed to easy overtime from weekends spent harassing hot dog vendors, contemplated the loss of income. Things were so bad at Queers Against Israeli Apartheid they couldn't even summon the courage to blame the Jews.

Oh, and that reminds me. . . . You know that application form for next year's grant money? Might as well recycle it now, dear, while they're still collecting the blue boxes.

Time to hand out the OxyContin

TUE NOV 9 2010
By: Chris Selley

The outrage in certain quarters at the Rob Ford campaign's postelection revelations has been a bit precious. In case you haven't heard: When the campaign learned that Mr. Ford had been caught on tape offering to help Dieter Doneit-Henderson score OxyContin (whoops, sorry, I just burst out laughing typing that sentence. Seriously, how amazing is it that Rob Ford is going to be mayor of Toronto?). Anyway, when the campaign learned about the tape and that the *Toronto Star* was sitting on it, deputy communications director Fraser Macdonald set out to win Mr. Doneit-Henderson's confidence, using a Twitter account he set up under the handle Queens-Quay Karen, aka Karen Philby, who was purportedly a George Smitherman supporter.

It's also since emerged that someone from Team

Ford, masquerading as the fictional Ms. Philby, called the John Tory show in July and urged him, rather rudely, not to run. This was part of a coordinated campaign to keep Mr. Tory out of the race, Mr. Kouvalis explained on Friday, when he and Mr. Smitherman's, Joe Pantalone's and Rocco Rossi's campaign directors sat down at a Public Affairs Association of Canada event and aired their dirty laundry.

Certainly it was a good idea to target Mr. Tory. Had he entered the race, it's safe to say Mr. Ford's chances would have been drastically slimmer.

But did they cross a line with their impersonations? "Did Ford campaign's tricks knock Tory out?" the *Star* asked. Mr. Tory scoffed at the notion, as you'd expect. The idea that a random phone call would convince a seasoned politician to stay out of the race, or for that matter that a *Star* story about the OxyContin affair— shoot, I'm giggling again—would have sunk a man who seemed to actually have been buoyed in the polls by a DUI conviction, is preposterous. This was no dirtier than politics as usual.

That doesn't make it right, of course. "I look at this stuff as being part of a much broader malaise infecting the political world right now," Mr. Tory said last week.

And that's the interesting thing. Mr. Ford capitalized on disdain for politicians even as his team partook of the tactics that contribute to it—and then they bragged about it. Why would practitioners of political dark arts reveal their magic? Especially when the magic is so garden-variety, and when convincing Mr. Tory not to run—which they probably didn't even do—was so integral, by their own admission, to their win? "I'll win you the election, sir, unless Joe Blow runs, in which case we're screwed," isn't exactly what I'd want to hear from my campaign manager.

Clearly, members of Team Ford are rather pleased with themselves, and I don't blame them. But partly, too, I suspect they're blabbing because they know how much uncontrollable events and dumb luck have to do with success and failure in political campaigns. If Rob Ford can win, anyone can, assuming they capture the zeitgeist as well. Better get your name out there when you're on a high.

But whatever the reason, I'm glad they're running their mouths. The more ugly behind-the-scenes information we have about politics, the more likely people will be to demand better.

No, I'm not angry at Don Cherry; It's Rob Ford who owes the city an apology

WED DEC 8 2010
By: Chris Selley

Don Cherry does strange things to people. He's been accused of "shifting . . . the meaning of hockey in Canadian life . . . from being emblematic of a culture of survival to an offshoot of the military"—quite the feat for someone who can't string a sentence together.

He's also been accused of "merrily pushing this country to the far right, loony division," by endorsing, in his free time, Julian Fantino for MP for Vaughan and Rob Ford for mayor of Toronto. And that's just one *Globe and Mail* columnist over the course of two months!

I've often lampooned Canadians' tendency to lose all sense of perspective when Grapes is part of the story. The guy's on television for, like, 20 minutes a week! But now, after Mr. Cherry's speech to city council on Tuesday, it seems to be my turn to blow a gasket.

I'm not angry at Mr. Cherry, mind you. He has a biological imperative to spout off about how virtuous he is and about how dreadfully hard done by he's been by "left-wing pinko newspapers." I'm angry at Mr. Ford for allowing him to become the main story of his first city council meeting as mayor.

I'd love to focus on Mr. Ford's beaming smile, the obvious delight with which he presided over the proceedings—so at odds with the morose, mumbling automaton of the campaign trail; on his sincere, friendly photo ops with councillors of all political stripes, all the way down to progressive stalwarts Gord Perks, Adam Vaughan and Glenn De Baeremaeker; on his heartfelt belly laugh when Mr. Perks fake punched him and Mr. De Baeremaeker kissed him on the cheek; on his on-message but not inflammatory speech, highlighted by an obviously heartfelt reference to the joys of public service.

But clearly he didn't want us to talk about that, because he invited Mr. Cherry to deliver a speech, and didn't stop him when he proceeded to insult giant swaths of the population of a city he doesn't even live in.

Offered a chance to comment afterwards, Mr. Ford claimed he hadn't known what Mr. Cherry would say— which is, admittedly, better than if he had. But there wasn't a hint of contrition. "I'm a huge fan of Don Cherry and *Coach's Corner*," he added. "And Don is exactly . . . what you see is what you get."

So, screw it. Let's talk about Don Cherry and his pink suit jacket and his offensive speech.

"I'm wearing pinko for all the pinkos out there that ride bicycles and everything," he began—one of his more intelligible utterances, despite doubling the number of syllables in the word "pink."

So, that's great. People who ride bicycles are communists—or at least worthy of investigation. (Goodness knows what "and everything" means. Hide your library cards, people.)

And then there was Mr. Cherry's memorable conclusion: "I say he's going to be the greatest mayor this city has ever seen, as far as I'm concerned, and put that in your pipe, you left-wing kooks."

I'm all for political incorrectness. But this was like Don Rickles without the laughs. Mr. Cherry berated the City of Toronto with a bitter, self-interested screed, and Mr. Ford followed with a speech about respect for taxpayers—all of them; about councillors working together to implement the enormous mandate for change handed them on Oct. 25; about a transportation plan that respected cyclists, for heaven's sake!

"Put that in your pipe, you left-wing kooks"? How can Mr. Ford just shrug when his invited guest spoke at such insulting cross-purposes to his own?

Like I said, Mr. Cherry was just doing what he does.

As I write this, I imagine he's at home in Mississauga, gently stroking his persecution complex while browsing the day's press clippings and counting his (taxpayer) money. It's Mr. Ford who owes the city an apology.

Don Cherry's Remarks

Rob Ford was sworn in as Mayor of Toronto on Tuesday at City Hall, and posed for photos with the 44 city councillors—one of whom, Glenn De Baeremaeker, jokingly kissed Mr. Ford on the cheek. The following remarks were then delivered by Don Cherry, who was wearing a pink suit jacket, at Mr. Ford's invitation.

That kiss—is that the kiss of death that they give like, ah, I guess that's what they do around here. Well actually I'm wearing pinko for all the pinkos out there that ride bicycles and everything. I thought I'd get it in. What'd you expect, Ron Maclean here, to come here? But, you know, I have to, I am befuddled, because I thought I was just doing a good thing coming down with Rob, and I was gonna do this here and it was gonna be nice and the whole deal. I'm been being ripped to shreds by the left-wing pinko newspapers out there. It's unbelievable. One guy called me a jerk in a pink suit, so I thought I'd wear that for him too, today. You know, it's funny, in those articles my church was, I was made fun of because I go to church. I'm easy to do it that way. I was called maudlin for the troops because I honour the troops. This is the kind of, uh, you're gonna be facing, Rob, with these left-wing pinkos. They scrape the bottom of the barrel. But again, I was asked why I was asked. And I asked Doug, Rob, why? And they said we need a famous good-looking guy, and I, I'm your man, right? Right off the bat. You know I was asked why, why, why a landslide. And I was in their corner right from the start. I phoned, they phoned me, Doug phoned me, the morning, you'll get a landslide, and why? Because Rob's honest, he's truthful, he's like Julian Fantino. What you see is what you get. He's no phony. And I could go on right now, all the millions and thousands of dollars he's gonna save and everything, but I'd just like to tell a little story that was in the *Sun*, I think it was in the back pages. This is a little thing. [City Ombudsman] Fiona Crean, for 18 months, has been trying to get something done with City Hall. And then the story, I think some of you know the story, that there was a little old lady and all of a sudden she got banged on the door, and two guys were there and said, "We're cutting your tree down." You know this is a little thing, but this is to me is a big thing. "We're cutting your tree down." And she says I don't want it, that's my favourite tree, a hundred year old. "No, it's down. Cut it down." And then they give her a, send her a bill for $5,000 for cutting it down. And for 18 months, her son and Fiona were, "City Hall, City Hall, please help us." Thirty, 40 calls. Unbelievable. Nothing. Laughed at. Rob's in the mayor one day. Apology comes, and a

$5,000 cheque. And that's why I say he's going to be the greatest mayor this city has ever seen, as far as I'm concerned, and put that in your pipe, you left-wing kooks. Thank you very much.

New police budget proves Ford's mettle

WED JAN 12 2011
By: Chris Selley

"Vote for Rob Ford—he'll put fewer cops on the streets!" It sounds like a campaign slogan from an alternate universe, and yet that's the likely effect of the Toronto Police Service operating budget proposal approved by the Police Services Board on Tuesday, with the mayor's support.

The net budget request of $905.9-million is 2% higher than last year, but $9-million lower than its original ask, which the mayor—who asked all departments to trim 5% from their budgets—greeted with notable displeasure. At a pugnacious Monday morning press conference, he wouldn't even confirm Chief Bill Blair's job security.

But now, everything's tickety-boo. "I had a very, very good discussion with the mayor yesterday," Chief Blair told reporters after the meeting. "We talked about a number of issues with respect to the city's finances and the police finances. We discussed some of the solutions that I was proposing, and I'm quite hopeful that we've been able to address the concerns that were raised."

Board vice-chairman and Councillor Michael Thompson said he thought the mayor would be "very pleased" by the plan, and so he is. "Public safety is paramount to Mayor Ford and he supports the Chief, the TPSB and the decisions that were made [Tuesday]," the mayor's office said in a statement.

The plan is simple: Don't hire anyone, uniformed or civilian, in 2011, for a savings of $7.6-million. (The other $1.4-million comes from requesting fewer reserve funds.) If that's approved, needless to say, there will at some point soon be fewer cops in Toronto. According to Chief Blair, 200 to 220 officers leave the force in an average year. We won't be down that many, as some new hires haven't yet hit their beats. But we'll certainly, eventually, be down.

File that under P for "previously unthinkable." And under H for "huzzah!" Mayor Ford generally supports the police to, and sometimes beyond, the ends of the earth. That he's on board with this strengthens his budget-cutting credibility enormously.

It's not that we necessarily need fewer police officers on the streets at any one time, although some argue that's the case. It's simply that the Toronto Police Service shouldn't be exempt from Mr. Ford's war on waste or his crusade for efficiencies just because it's the Toronto Police Service. If the police can save $1.9-million on overtime, court appearances and other premium pay without impacting service—which everyone swears blind this budget will not—then why the heck wouldn't they? Why not spend $9,000 less on advertising, $400,000 less on conferences and seminars, $100,000 less on contracted services?

Also on Tuesday, the Police Services Board voted to ask the city to "pursue the feasibility of contracting out custodial and maintenance services for all police facilities." Estimates of possible savings from such a move run around $500,000 annually. "Why haven't we done this before?" asked new board member Dr. Dhun Noria, sounding genuinely confused. If it was a planted question, she delivered it well. The answer, of course, is because the old regime was ideologically allergic to the idea, and the new one, thank goodness, isn't.

A hiring freeze isn't an efficiency, of course. An efficiency would be delivering the same service as before with fewer people. And there's no shortage of ideas as to how to do that: Former mayor John Sewell, for example, believes restructuring officers' work weeks could effectively fill the gap created by a year with no hires.

These are precisely the conversations every city department should be having—not because it's good to have fewer cops or to put unionized cleaners out of work, but because everyone agrees we're pretty much broke and senior levels of government aren't particularly inclined, for whatever reason, to help us out. Even if the poo hits the fan a year from now, as many predict, and taxes have to rise or major services cut to keep Mr. Ford's agenda afloat, it should have been a hugely worthwhile exercise going forward.

Ford called out on his promises

MON JAN 31 2011
By: Matt Gurney and Jonathan Goldsbie

Contrary to the expectation of many, including no doubt most people who voted for Rob Ford, the city will actually employ more people in the first year of Ford's administration. After all the claims about waste at City Hall and lambasting of those officials who'd allowed Toronto's workforce to balloon under David Miller, Matt Gurney and Jonathan Goldsbie ask how Ford's hiring of even more workers sits with the citizens.

GOLDSBIE: City press releases conclude with a paragraph of boilerplate, offering basic background information on the City of Toronto and its leadership. As of Jan. 5, the text was modified to reflect Mayor Rob Ford's particular priorities, including the self-cannibalistic pledge that "Toronto's government is dedicated to . . . reducing the size and cost of government." It's therefore amusingly ironic that this year's city budgets involve a net increase of 48 jobs, rather than the mass shrinkage Ford repeatedly promised during the campaign. But I'm not terribly fond of mocking him for breaking a vow that was poorly thought out in the first place; while I enjoy watching reality smash apart his dishonest rhetoric, I also believe in positive reinforcement. Capital projects such as making TTC stations accessible necessarily require hiring new people to get the job done. On the one hand, good for him for (in this narrow case) not placing ideology ahead of progress. On the other hand, wouldn't you say that's a rather low bar for governance?

GURNEY: I'd grant that that's a low bar for governance, but wouldn't grant that Ford is only reaching that unenviable target. As to the crux of the issue, while some of Ford's all-anger/no-brains supporters might be outraged, I believe that most Ford supporters—and voters who didn't vote for him but conceivably might—won't be too freaked out by what is essentially a rounding error in the city's workforce. I think the Ford team has been pretty clear that 2011 was going to be a year where not a whole lot changed while the new government got a handle on the nitty gritty details of the city's operations. I entirely agree with something Chris Selley (who couldn't join us today) recently said in a column: Bring in outsider auditors, get a handle on every department and agency, and go from there. That might mean that 2012 is indeed a year of painful cuts, or if a full audit dragged on, Ford might content himself with largely holding the line until ready to make big sweeping moves on staffing levels. What did catch my eye was Doug Holyday's comments that, having now taken office, they're going to have to reconsider which of their promises they can follow through on. That's pragmatic to a degree and in a sense refreshing to hear, but I was a bit unnerved to see how quickly they seemed to be backing away from major job cuts. Having an election promise arrive later than expected, that's something the voters need to be grown up about. But a Reduce the Size of Government Campaign can't go back on a promise to slash the government without warranting some backlash.

GOLDSBIE: The paradox of Ford is that he ran both a Reduce the Size of Government Campaign and a Make People Happy Campaign and didn't quite understand that there might be a contradiction there. While some people (yourself included) are of the belief that small government is an ideal in itself, I do like to think that's a minority opinion and that most people understand that government of a certain stature is fundamental to the quality of life we enjoy and would like to build upon. But regardless of who's in charge, 2012 was always going to be an especially difficult budget, with the bills for a number of capital projects coming due. The solution hinted at by Councillor Doug Ford (who functions as both the de facto mayor and the de facto budget chief) seems to be the privatization of whatever assets can be legally jettisoned . . . but even setting aside the debate around whether that is wise or desirable, there is no reason to think that it would be anything less than extremely difficult to achieve and that, even if achieved, it would result in any substantial savings. Every once in a while, Rob and Doug will open their mouths, and I am unnervingly reminded that they don't understand their populist grandstanding is exactly that. Government is an infinitely more complex organism than newspapers and talk radio portray it to be, and it is resistant to easy answers. I can only hope that as the Fords gradually come to appreciate that fact, their response is not a vicious one.

Ford fails credibility test; Taking hard line on police would send a message

FRI MAY 13 2011
By: Matt Gurney

The raise for Toronto's police force, announced last week, is more than just another costly promise made by a city government deep in debt and facing a huge budgetary shortfall next year. It is a missed political opportunity for Mayor Rob Ford, one he won't get again. Taking a hard line on the raise for police would have sent a clear message to the city's unions—if the famously pro-police Fords are willing to stand up for the taxpayers even against their beloved police officers, obviously these Ford boys mean business.

But that ship has sailed, and sunk. The 11.2% raise (over four years) the city has agreed to will not only cost nearly an annual $100-million once fully implemented, it also has essentially torpedoed any chance the city might have had to take a firm stance against the other unions, especially those deemed essential services.

Essential services, in giving up the right to strike, are awarded new contracts by an arbitrator if a new negotiated settlement can't be reached. Thanks to the police contract, the new "going rate" for essential service contracts is now 11.2% over four years.

Councillor Adam Vaughan called it a rookie mistake, and he's right. But the real mistake can't be measured simply in dollars and cents, but in lost political credibility. When the city does eventually attempt to tackle its spending problems, it will be left in the awkward spot of trying to explain why one essential service is worth more than another. In Toronto, apparently, not everything essential will be deemed equally essential.

From a practical basis, it's not hard to figure out why. At the risk of oversimplifying, for the city's right-wing councillors, unions are bad, except when they're first responders. Then they're great.

There's a certain logic to it—not every unionized member of the city's workforce shoulders the same burdens and takes the same risks as first responders, who are rightfully lauded for their unique contributions to society.

But however understandable, such favouritism just won't do when it's coming from the government of the city, which holds a duty to both the taxpayers and the city's unions to be competent, fair managers. Sometimes that means being tougher on the people you like than would be ideal, not because it's fun, but because leadership requires tough decisions.

Police Board chairman Alok Mukherjee has said some of the blame must go to Queen's Park, which has inflated labour contracts across the province.

He has a point. But he also misses the point: It may well have been inevitable that Toronto's finest were going to get a big raise. What wasn't inevitable was the Ford administration willingly giving up so much of its fiscal credibility at the same time.

Ford on a float would be nice

FRI JUN 24 2011
By: Chris Selley

What would Toronto be without its annual Pride morality play? Queers Against Israeli Apartheid is anti-Semitic. No, it's free speech. No, it's hate speech. You can say whatever you want, just not with public money. City Hall shouldn't fund parades, period. There's too much nudity—it's obscene and illegal. No, you're just homophobic. Why do they have to make being homosexual such an enormous part of their identity? I don't march in a "straight pride" parade. Yeah, but you don't know what it's like to be discriminated against.

Everyone gets to stake out their moral turf and preen, like a peacock unfurling its plumage. And Mayor Rob Ford's decision not to attend this year's Pride Parade on July 3 has some of us practically bursting with righteous indignation. It proves he's homophobic. It proves he's a jerk. It proves he's mayor of certain constituencies in Toronto, but not of others.

There might be something to the latter point. It would be nice to see Mr. Ford at the parade for a few reasons, most notably because one expects to see the mayor of any city at one of its biggest yearly events. It would be nice to see him respond to the unremitting, infantile personal attacks against him by certain quarters of the left—*NOW* magazine readers, for lack of a better shorthand—by cruising down Yonge Street at the city's most liberal event, smiling and throwing a water balloon or two. Frankly, it would just be nice to see Mr. Ford smile. He famously described himself as "300 pounds of fun," but his City Hall is a pretty dour place.

And having decided not to go, it would have been nice if he'd said something other than, basically, "I have to go to the cottage." It implies he'd go to Pride if he was in town, which invites an examination of the hardship involved in coming down from Huntsville for the day— he could probably be back in time for dinner—which in turn invites questions about his priorities. It makes the decision seem more consequential than it really is.

Is Mr. Ford homophobic? A few moronic outbursts notwithstanding, I see no reason to think so. His reputation as a sort of minor league all-purpose bigot is baffling when compared with his record as a municipal politician: He obsessively solves people's problems, no matter who they are. This is a man who wouldn't hang up on a dude trying to score OxyContin. So the idea that riding a float at Pride would change anyone's mind about Mr. Ford is laughable in the first place. Many of the people professing "disappointment" at his decision this week were clearly overjoyed to have an opportunity to hate him even more.

Mel Lastman was quoted on Thursday encouraging Mr. Ford to attend the parade, recalling his own initial reluctance and that he quickly learned to enjoy it— despite a few too many "bare asses." But Mr. Lastman was a cheerleader for Toronto. He was a happy sales- man, a grinning bungler. Mr. Ford, when he's not flying off the handle, can appear painfully unsure of himself in public.

Maybe he's just uncomfortable around naked strangers. Most of us are, 364 days of the year. That's not inherently homophobic. It's normal.

Ultimately, if he wanted to make it, he'd make it. It's somewhat disappointing that he won't, and it's reasonable to argue that sexual politics aside, he has a minor obligation to be there. But the reaction has been far too overwrought, and too giddy, to take seriously— especially since this was the most predictable outcome. A real expression of pride, surely, would be not to worry about a guy you don't much like anyway not showing up. Here's hoping he crashes next year's party and blows some minds.

Proud to skip Pride

Fri Jun 24 2011
By: Barbara Kay

Toronto Mayor Rob Ford is not going to march in the Pride Parade this year because the date of the parade conflicts with his lifetime tradition of spending Canada Day weekend at his family's Muskoka cottage. "I've been going to Huntsville as long as I can remember," Mr. Ford said. "Since I was a little boy, we always used to go up north to our cottage, and I'm carrying on the tradition that my father had."

Good for Rob Ford. Canada Day is a day for all Canadians to celebrate their nation as a 34-million strong collective, not a small minority of people celebrating their sexuality. There are times when family trumps political work, and this is, or should be, inarguably one of them.

Mr. Ford's decision should have been accepted with good grace, especially since he reassured everyone this was an exception to the rule. Instead, his opponents took the low road, implying that his perfectly reasonable decision was a deliberate insult to gays, for which Mr. Ford would have to "make amends." Councillor Kristen Wong-Tam, whose ward is heavily populated with gays, called it a "grave mistake," because it "sends the wrong message to the [lesbian, gay, bisexual and transgender] community." Councillor Janet Davis said that Mr. Ford was sending a clear message that members of the LGBT "don't count in Rob Ford's city."

The knives that are out for Mr. Ford have nothing to do with this particular decision, though. The exaltation of homosexuality is second only to the reverence paid to unfettered abortion as a litmus test for political correctness amongst our cognitive and cultural elites. Rob Ford's sin is that he does not believe in mixing politics with sexuality pride. Rob Ford is not a homophobe, but nor on the other hand does he think it is any particular honour to be homosexual. Many Canadians not schooled in the catechism of gender correctness agree with him.

His shameful rap sheet includes the fact that he did not march in the parade while he was a councillor— that's 10 whole years of not marching—and he has even had the temerity to argue against using city money for this (or any other) special-interest parade. It is too bad that certain members of the gay community reflexively take a zero-sum attitude to any politician's perceived lack of support. This incident is instructive. Francisco Alvarez, co-chair of Pride Toronto, said Mr. Ford's absence is a missed opportunity to "strengthen his connection with the LGBT community," and added rather ominously, that "if he never comes, well, I guess we can draw conclusions about that."

In other words, if a politician is there, he is a friend to the gays. If he doesn't march, he isn't neutral in his feelings about gays; he must be a homophobe. Mr. Ford's instincts were absolutely right when he argued against funding the Pride Parade. Undoubtedly he will be asked to walk in the next Slut Walk parade. I doubt that Mr. Ford thinks that a woman's right to dress and act like women whose business it is to arouse lust and get paid for satisfying it is a cause worth giving up a weekend in Muskoka for. Or giving up a single precious moment doing anything else for. But you can be sure that if he is asked and refuses, he will be castigated by women's groups as a sexist.

Pierre Elliott Trudeau said that the government should stay out of the bedrooms of the nation. He did not foresee that once the closet doors were opened wide, the bedrooms of the nations would spill over to occupy the streets of every major city in Canada. He did not foresee the day when politicians would almost literally be dragged into those bedrooms and forced to admire the antics going on therein.

Pride has no more legal and political ambitions to fulfil. The revolution is over. Pride is no longer about "support" for gays. Now it's all about having gay-themed fun. They don't need politicians for that. Some Pride participants do everything but have actual sex in public, and if tourists want to make the trip to see that, so be it.

Pride doesn't need public money, any more than strip shows do. Millions of tolerant, non-homophobic Canadians find nothing to celebrate in lewd self-promotion. Rob Ford is one of them, I assume. He would do everyone a favour if he never marched in another Pride Parade again. I bet there are hundreds of other politicians in Canada who secretly wished they had the nerve to follow suit.

Is Rob Ford showing pride or prejudice?

TUE JUN 28 2011

By: Jonathan Goldsbie, Matt Gurney and Chris Selley

Rob Ford—homophobic, shy or incoherent? In this week's Posted Toronto Political Panel, Jonathan Goldsbie, Matt Gurney and Chris Selley discuss the mayor's ongoing Pride saga.

GOLDSBIE: Rob Ford doesn't care about gay people. To infer anything else from his increasingly egregious series of statements, actions and snubs is to engross oneself in a severe state of denial. Oh sure, he probably cares about a gay person—I have no reason to doubt his brother's assurances that Rob will assist an individual constituent regardless of his or her race, ethnicity, sexuality, etc. But at this point, it is clear that gay people make him uncomfortable. And this wouldn't even be such a problem if he made an effort to at least pretend this were not the case. The mayor, however, has never demonstrated any inclination toward adapting or evolving as a person or as a leader; there he sits, in an awkward limbo, unable to reject his own prejudices but unable to explicitly concede them, either. Perhaps he doesn't grasp the gravity of his very public dilemma, or perhaps he is waiting for it all to blow over. But is there any way he doesn't come across as, at minimum, a coward?

SELLEY: Let's face it: You infer all of the foregoing because it fits with your preconceived notions of the guy and because it delights you to stick one more feather on Ford's tar-covered frame. Other reasons he might not want to go include stubbornness—especially once he said no to the parade, the press freaked out, and everyone started lining up to offer their advice like he's 19 years old; a well-founded fear of being treated badly by people like you, who already thought he was homophobic, not to mention every other kind of evil; and just garden variety incoherence. Why does he support spending taxpayer money to subsidize a dinky little ski hill? Why is he spending so much political capital promising to build a subway along Sheppard when the people it would serve will have to move there to make it financially viable? Beats the hell out of me. Personally, I think he should march on the principle that a mayor should appear at his city's marquee events. And I have no idea why he's letting this situation simmer. But I don't think it's going to change anyone's mind about the guy one way or the other.

GURNEY: I find it interesting that Jonathan is willing to concede that the mayor would care about a gay person, but also implies that that's not good enough. Why isn't it? If Pride is about equality and celebrating the strides that have been made by Canadian homosexuals (and all the others that Pride encompasses), isn't a belief that Mayor Ford would treat a homosexual, bisexual or transgendered citizen the same as any other proof of Pride's enormous victory? I agree with Chris that he should go, because it's his job and it would spare him political grief. And I agree with Jonathan enough to grant that Ford doesn't seem comfortable about Pride (though saying he's therefore uncomfortable with gay people period is a stretch, unless we accept that Pride is universally recognized as an entirely faithful microcosm of "what it is" to be gay). The question I have is if we all agree that Ford would treat a gay person with total fairness and equality . . . isn't that a sign that the worthy goals of Pride—respect and equal treatment for homosexuals—have been accomplished, at least as concerns a Mr. Rob Ford?

Price to pay for cuts to police, fire department

SAT OCT 8 2011
By: Christie Blatchford

As Rick Hillier, the former Canadian chief of the defence staff, once famously said, "We're not the public service of Canada. We're not just another government department. We are the Canadian Forces, and our job is to be able to kill people."

I've been thinking of General Hillier, and that fabulous (and accurate) quote, for the past several weeks, as the machinations among Toronto Police Chief Bill Blair, his board and Mayor Rob Ford have become increasingly public, and as I learned about the much more private, but comparable, battle going on between the mayor and the Toronto fire department.

In a nutshell, Mayor Ford, who used to brag that one of his first acts of office would be to give Chief Blair, unsolicited, a whack of new officers (the Chief declined), is now demanding that the force, like every other city department, like the fire department, must cut its budget by 10%.

Mayor Ford, who rode to power on an end-the-gravy-train-at-City-Hall platform, appears to be married to such across-all-department cuts—though it was under his watch, in fact, that the police board negotiated a cunning four-year deal with the police association that gives them an 11% raise and will add almost $25-million a year to the cost of policing the country's largest city.

The mayor's great pal on city council and a police board member, Michael Thompson, was this week behaving like a thug, actually publicly threatening Chief Blair's job if he didn't come to heel; the board chair, Alok Mukherjee, under whose auspices that sweetheart deal was reached and who has presided over hearty growth in policing costs, has suddenly converted to Mayor Ford's thrifty ways; reporters, sensing blood, have moved in for the kill.

But the mayor's across-the-board economies are false because, like the Canadian Forces, the police department isn't just another branch of the government, interchangeable with the folks at parks and rec or social services or the libraries Torontonians love so dearly.

To paraphrase General Hillier, the copper's job is to protect people and keep the streets safe, and to do it, he or she carries a gun and is legally allowed to use lethal force.

It is unfashionable to mention, but there's also a sense of calling which motivates many police officers, certainly all of the best of them. They are part of what the former U.S. Army Lieutenant-Colonel Dave Grossman calls "the sheepdogs," those few who want to protect the sheep, which is most of the rest of us, from the other few, the societal predators he calls wolves.

So are firefighters and paramedics part of that group? They are there to save you when you've set the bed afire, carry you out through flames, rush you to hospital, and treat your hurts and injuries.

These are all people-heavy departments, with wages and benefits eating up much of the budget: Mayor Ford's 10% solution invariably means layoffs, which is precisely what Chief Blair has told them—though the board members appear to have willed themselves deaf.

What's happening in the fire department is instructive.

At its full complement, the service has 3,183 people, including those in administration. It is already 91 people short—the last recruit class was abruptly cancelled in July—and at least 65 of those are, as Toronto Professional Firefighters' Association president Ed Kennedy put it this week, "from the trucks."

What it has meant, as both Mr. Kennedy and Toronto Fire Chief Bill Stewart confirm—is that the department has trucks out of service on an almost daily basis already.

And in two recent fatal fires—one in late August on

Rogers Road in the west end, the other this month on Huron Street in the core—the second truck at two different two-truck stations was out of service because of staff shortages.

Trucks from other stations, located farther away, had to respond, and while Chief Stewart says "response times were good, there's no question when we have to bring apparatus in [from farther away], we're going to get longer response times."

As Mr. Kennedy told me, speaking of the Huron Street fire, "Seconds—not minutes, seconds—can make a difference [in saving lives]. Whether or not it made a difference in this case, I don't know. But there's going to be others."

Chief Stewart, sounding beat up, said, "If we're not in a position to replace staff, we're going to take more trucks out of service on a daily basis.

"I've articulated that [to the city manager] in writing. At the end of the day, it's about public safety. I don't know where it's going to end. I don't know what the hell we do."

In the old days, it was understood that cops, firefighters and paramedics were different, and they weren't held to the same hiring restrictions and cutbacks as other departments. Now they are, and for all the posturing to the contrary, there's a price to be paid.

These men and women don't deal with widgets,

numbers, charts, swimming pools and slides or books, but with life and death, loss and human suffering. It's from the ranks of us sheep, in other words, where the toll will be extracted.

Nothing funny in accosting mayor; CBC prank shows bad taste, signs of squeal culture

SAT OCT 29 2011
By: Christie Blatchford

Uncharacteristically, I've been listening to CBC Radio a little these days.

Normally, but for *Hockey Night in Canada* and *The National*, I don't pay much heed to the Mother Corp., period. I work part time for a private radio station in Toronto, so I listen to it for news, and when it's music I want, I'm a Q-107 girl all the way.

But since I have temporarily relocated to Kingston, where I'm covering the "honour killings" trial, I've had the radio in my bedroom turned to CBC, and find it generally useful for inducing a restful sleep.

Thus it was one night this week, I was drifting off to Jian Ghomeshi's show, *Q*.

It begins with a short monologue, and on Wednesday night, Mr. Ghomeshi devoted it to his thoughts on the nationally infamous Rob Ford run-in earlier in the week with Mary Walsh, one of the stars (I do use the word loosely) of CBC TV's *This Hour Has 22 Minutes.*

Ms. Walsh, allegedly nationally famous for her role as Marg Delahunty, or Marg, Princess Warrior, had bearded the Toronto mayor early Monday morning at his home. Mr. Ford was apparently about to take his little daughter, who was just inside the door, to school. He was alarmed and taken by surprise; his daughter, he says, was scared.

Mr. Ford has received serious death threats before, and back he went in the house to call 911.

So that's the background, if, by some miracle, you missed it in the unending coverage this week.

"Oh dear, Rob Ford," Mr. Ghomeshi began, and went on to chide the mayor for not knowing the "first rule of politics—play along with the satirists," agreeing that approaching him at his home was rough but adding, "This is Mary Walsh we're talking about, Marg, Princess Warrior."

He pointed out that Ms. Walsh has ambushed other politicians (mind you, few, if any, that I could find at their homes). Why, they could take a joke, he said, though in fact, when I watched the video on the CBC website, I thought most of them, but for Stephen Harper, looked profoundly uncomfortable.

The inference was huge: Mr. Ford bloody ought to have known who Ms. Walsh was (the show, Mr. Ghomeshi said, is a "national institution" and has been on the air since 1993) and is surely an out-of-touch rube, and a humourless one at that.

But then, he concluded sadly with that special knowingness of CBC hosts, this is the "new Toronto," where creative expression is stifled, to which I'd say that may be so, but what has creative expression to do with *22 Minutes*?

Now, in the days since Mr. Ghomeshi's monologue that night, CBC has reported that Mr. Ford swore during one or another of his 911 calls, allegedly called the dispatcher a "bitch," and that "multiple sources" say the dispatchers were upset. He has denied saying bitch (which Toronto Police Chief Bill Blair confirmed Friday, saying he had listened to a tape of the call), but admitted swearing.

CBC News then ran a poll asking if listeners thought Mr. Ford should apologize, and Ms. Walsh and the show have had more ink than they have in years.

Where to begin? First, I think, with the show.

I watched it once or twice, years ago, and found it profoundly unfunny. I have since watched online Ms. Walsh in her greatest hits as Marg: Princess Warrior, and I have to say I find her particularly unfunny. (A clue: Her Wikipedia biography describes her as "an actress, comedian and social activist," a combination I consider oxymoronic and inherently incompatible.) In fact, Ms. Walsh may be the only unfunny person I have ever seen from Newfoundland, which produces more wildly amusing people than any other province.

In other words, if Ms. Walsh had turned up at my house—either in Toronto or Kingston—early in the morn, wearing that costume and brandishing a plastic sword, I would not have had a clue who she was, and might have sicced my dog on her. (Well, alright, I might have if I had a dog who could be sicced upon people. Mine can't be. I don't think I'd have called 911, but then, I wouldn't have had a little kid in the wings.)

Ms. Walsh has, in the aftermath of all this, described herself as "a 60-year-old woman with a plastic sword," as if only a ninny could have been alarmed by such an apparition.

Well, as another 60-year-old who occasionally catches unanticipated glimpses of herself, sans sword, I can assure you it can be frightening.

Secondly, while I've found Mr. Ford's first year in office often disappointing and graceless, as exemplified by his inability to make an easy gesture during Pride Week, I'm with him on this one.

As for the purportedly upset dispatchers—CBC's *The National*, flogging the already really dead horse, reported Thursday night that the dispatchers were so concerned they had a meeting with their union—my advice would be to grow a thicker skin.

If you sign up for a job where people by definition will call you in various states of panic, despair and fear—often where there has been injury, death or illness—you had better be able to handle the occasional curse word without feeling disrespected.

I would also say that the CBC, as a newsgathering organization, has been both breathless and condescending about what is a terribly inside-baseball story about one of their own.

Finally, the entire business seems to me to stand as a marker for the squeal culture now rampant in the country's biggest city.

One half of Torontonians seem to refuse to ever talk to the police, refuse to come forward as witnesses to serious crime or testify in court; the other half phone someone, the press or the police, if they see Mr. Ford on his cell in his car.

There's a happy medium in there somewhere. It may well be in Kingston.

"No reason to continue silly *Star* vendetta"

MON DEC 5 2011
By: Jonathan Goldsbie and Chris Selley

With Matt Gurney off at ultimate fighting camp, Jonathan Goldsbie and Chris Selley have a totally unbiased conversation about the Ford brothers' battle with the Toronto Star.

GOLDSBIE: On Friday, Rob Ford published a fantastically misleading statement on Facebook: "There have been some comments made recently regarding access to information from the mayor's office and the *Toronto Star*. . . . To be perfectly clear, the *Toronto Star* receives all notifications, press releases, media advisories from the City of Toronto." Well, yes, they do—anyone can sign up to the email list to which the City of Toronto's Strategic Communications Division distributes general news releases regarding City business. What is at issue, and what the *Star* is being denied, is inclusion on the separate email list to which the office of the mayor sends out its own notifications, press releases and media advisories: the mayor's statements on public matters, as well as bulletins informing the press of where and when he will be speaking to them. It's all pretty basic stuff that the mayor, who legally serves as the city's chief executive officer and is therefore bound to represent the government itself, should disseminate without discrimination. And yet this has become one of those contentious issues, not unlike his participation in Pride, in which he refuses to set aside his own prejudices for the sake of his duty. Is there any legitimate reason for Rob Ford to continue to allow his stubbornness to trump all else?

SELLEY: You're damn good at fanning flames, Jonathan. A little throwaway line about Rob Ford being a proven homophobe—shouldn't council at least get a vote on that?—sours an otherwise perfectly sensible point. But no, there's no reason for the mayor to continue this silly vendetta, which is of no practical effect anyway: No one's really out of the loop in the press gallery no matter what's in their inbox. But nor, frankly, do I see any reason for the *Star* to pursue this with the Integrity Commissioner or publish article after article about their battle with the Fords: They're well within their rights, and since Ford let his libel suit against the paper lapse, he doesn't have a legal or procedural leg to stand on. But what's the point of it all? To get some scrum notices at the same time as everyone else, instead of 60 seconds later? As I say, the *Star*'s in the right here. But I can't help thinking the cumulative effect of all this is to escalate a culture war that on most fronts has been calming down. I just wish it would go away.

GOLDSBIE: I meant "prejudice" in the "intractable preconceived notion of discomfort" sense, but I figure we'll have other opportunities to explore that nuance. (Perhaps in late spring.) The practical effect of the freeze-out actually does involve the *Star* occasionally missing events. As Dave Rider, the paper's Urban Affairs Bureau chief, explained on Councillor Josh Matlow's radio show Sunday, there are times when other gallery members forget to forward the notices and he only finds out about a press conference when he sees it carried live on CP24. I don't think the *Star* should be expected to put up with that, when the wrong is bound so tightly to a neglect of both legal and moral responsibilities. It's not entirely clear what the *Star* hopes the Integrity Commissioner will do about the matter (I think they'd actually have better luck convincing a court to issue a writ of mandamus), nor do I think it's especially tasteful for the paper to relish being the subject of its own news. But if, as Postmedia reported, the only contemporary examples of comparable behaviour originate in Indonesia and Mauritius, then, yeah, it's worth challenging through whatever avenues are available.

SELLEY: The irony, of course, is that the major journalistic advantage to being at a Rob Ford press conference is that you won't miss out on the opportunity to have your question not answered. Usually by Doug Ford. Watching Doug run point with all media last week on the fact that his brother won't talk to one outlet was downright hilarious. As the *Star* never tires of telling us, its reporters are still getting scoops and exclusives and the little day-to-day stories too, and I can't think of a one that would have been enriched by an official comment from His Worship. This goes for most good political reporting in most Canadian jurisdictions, incidentally. Now might actually be a good time for the media to consider just how much ink they spill repeating, verbatim, the complete nonsense that comes out of politicians' mouths. But the principle of the thing is the principle of the thing, and again, the *Star*'s in the right. They should get the bloody press notices. I just don't think this whole thing is . . . you know, news. (Yes, I am aware of the irony of us writing this for a newspaper.)

GOLDSBIE: I certainly think the frontpage story about Doug Ford trying to bring UFC (Ultimate Fighting Championship) to schools would have been enriched by a comment from him explaining that that's not what he was actually doing.

SELLEY: A valuable lesson learned—probably not.

The big deal behind Ford suit

Thu Nov 15 2012
By: Christie Blatchford

It was one sweet, sweet deal that George Foulidis got for himself—finally—in the summer of 2010.

Against the recommendations of its own staff and a purported civic push for transparency that ought to have put the kibosh on untendered contracts like Mr. Foulidis's, the City of Toronto and the 53-year-old signed a lease agreement that June 22.

The deal allowed Mr. Foulidis, whose $6-million lawsuit against Toronto Mayor Rob Ford is now being heard at Ontario Superior Court, to run the same Board-walk Café he'd operated for the two previous decades.

But he also got a few other things thrown in the mix.

For one thing, the size of the prime city-owned waterfront property that was his domain now expanded to include another city park, meaning he had exclusive food and beverage rights for the entire east beaches.

For another, Mr. Foulidis now also had exclusive

rights to sell suntan lotion and hats and the like, and received some revenue from the adjacent city-owned parking lot, all of which seems rather a long way from running a restaurant. As Gavin Tighe, Mr. Ford's lawyer, put it once during his cross-examination Wednesday, "You were the only game in town."

Mr. Foulidis also wangled "exclusive sponsorship rights" for the whole schmear, the meaning and value of which isn't clear from the evidence but which appears to involve money that would come to Mr. Foulidis for advertising or promotion. As well, it appears he had control over most of the special-event permits granted to other park users.

For all this, over the 20-year term of the lease, Mr. Foulidis agreed to pay the city $4.75-million—the rent, as it were—a whole $250,000 more than he had paid over the course of his previous 20-year lease.

So it really was a splendid deal, from his perspective, and clearly Mr. Foulidis is one smart, savvy and aggressive businessman.

The problem is, that's not what Mr. Ford—or a handful of others, for that matter—had to say about Mr. Foulidis, back two years ago in the swing of the election campaign that saw Mr. Ford elected.

Not surprisingly, the Boardwalk Café deal had become a hot potato—the then local councillor, Sandra Bussin, had gone to bat for the project—as indeed it had been occasionally for several years before.

There were murmurings about links between Mr. Foulidis and Ms. Bussin's campaign.

Indeed, he has admitted in testimony before Judge John Macdonald that over the years he sometimes donated to her campaign and sometimes didn't, on that occasion precisely because his deal was before council and he knew the "optics" might be bad.

He said he encouraged his family, friends and staff to donate too, and at that time, there were stories in the *Toronto Sun* about restaurant employees who had given the individual maximum—$750—even though they didn't live in the ward. But Mr. Foulidis denied he was strong-arming anyone or doing anything wrong.

Mr. Ford was then campaigning on a clean-up-City-Hall, stop-the-gravy-train theme, and the Boardwalk deal caught his attention.

As Mr. Foulidis said on Wednesday, it was as though his deal had become "the litmus test for lack of transparency" and all that Mr. Ford believed was wrong with city government.

He slammed it in a *Toronto Sun* editorial-board meeting—later reported on in the paper in August of 2010—as stinking "to high heaven" and smacking of civic corruption.

Now, Mr. Foulidis has a thick skin. Others, including a city councillor, had said much the same thing; newspaper columnists and talk-show hosts had criticized his deal and his dealings; Bruce Baker, a candidate for the ward where the Boardwalk Café is located and whom Mr. Foulidis is also suing here for defamation, had sent council a confidential letter asking for a police investigation.

But Mr. Ford's remarks were different, he said.

"I was very hurt by that article," he said in examination-in-chief by his lawyer, Brian Shiller. "I was humiliated. I felt like a criminal."

It was bad enough, Mr. Foulidis said, that Mr. Baker was denouncing him to "my landlord"—the city with whom he was dealing—but "Mr. Ford announced corruption to the world. My friends, family, everybody read it."

To give him full marks, Mr. Foulidis behaved then just as an innocent man likely would, too: Shortly after Mr. Ford's remarks were published in the *Sun*, he held a press conference of his own.

"I wanted to declare publicly that I had done nothing wrong," he said. "I wanted Mr. Ford to apologize, or bring forth evidence of corruption. I was overwhelmed by the allegations of criminality. . . . I felt I had to stand up for myself."

He's a proud man, Mr. Foulidis, with real dignity. He was clearly overwhelmed—not weeping or hamming it up, but struggling to speak—all over again as he testified, remembering the day his 10-year-old daughter "asked me if I had done anything wrong."

"How did that make you feel?" Mr. Shiller asked.

"Worse," Mr. Foulidis replied, "than I feel right now."

It is common ground at the trial that the two men—Rob Ford and George Foulidis—never met back then.

They didn't know one another; they are both family men, with kids; both businessmen. Both even have their brothers—Doug Ford for Mr. Ford, Danny Foulidis for Mr. Foulidis—in court at their respective sides.

They had never met. "That's what makes this even more outrageous," Mr. Foulidis said. They had never met, "yet he was willing to sacrifice my name, my reputation, all for political gain."

The case continues all week.

The viper's nest that is city politics

FRI NOV 16 2012
By: Christie Blatchford

The Rob Ford defamation trial now going on before Ontario Superior Court Judge John Macdonald here is nowhere near over, but one sharp lesson has emerged already: Don't enter municipal politics unless you have the stomach for it.

Mr. Ford, the Toronto mayor and coach of the Don Bosco Eagles football team, is being sued for $6-million by George Foulidis, a 53-year-old businessman who appears to have charmed or otherwise bamboozled the pants off the corporate entity that is the City of Toronto.

Mr. Foulidis is enjoying his second 20-year lease with the city to run a restaurant—and just about everything else on the eastern beaches, including exclusive rights to sell suntan lotion—on prime waterfront parkland the municipality owns.

With the first lease, he replied to a Request for Proposal from the city; with the second, signed just two years ago and due to expire in 2030, Mr. Foulidis submitted an unsolicited proposal and, after almost a decade of effort, won the day.

There were no competing bids because city council, over the objections of its own staff and against the prevailing trend to tender contracts, approved Mr. Foulidis's proposal. As he said Thursday, completing his testimony, "I followed the process that was available to me. I didn't create it."

It's a great synopsis: If the deal stinks, as Mayor Ford and others have said, the guilty party is the city.

In any event, it's this lease—and what Mr. Ford, then campaigning for the top job, and Bruce Baker, another candidate in the 2010 municipal election, allegedly had to say about it and about Mr. Foulidis—that is at the nub of the case.

Friday, Mr. Ford, his Eagles playing a big game Thursday, will testify.

So Mr. Baker, who is being sued by Mr. Foulidis for $100,000, went first, and it was through his evidence that a glimpse of the viper's nest that is municipal politics—and the utter casualness with which, in the nest, reputations are sullied—began to emerge.

Now 61, Mr. Baker lives in Ward 32, the area that encompasses the eastern Beach and Mr. Foulidis's restaurant.

A Grade 8 dropout, he has had varied careers, and is a former executive assistant to Councillor Ron Moeser, a former TTC subway driver and a former realtor. He now works doing research for his brother, lawyer Gordon Baker.

Mr. Baker is being sued for a letter he sent to city councillors and then-mayor David Miller in May of 2010.

Council was that very day to review the matter of Mr. Foulidis's lease—yet again.

Mr. Baker had just received an email from a friend, forwarding a letter he'd got from someone else, a man who purported to know Mr. Foulidis well and who announced that Mr. Foulidis had "repeatedly" told him "how he manages to obtain favours from Toronto City Hall in connection with his lease in the Beaches" and that "he pays, directly or indirectly, the key people."

(This man, incidentally, had been involved in previous litigation with Mr. Foulidis or his family, and had an axe to grind. Apparently, he has also been formally declared by a court to be a vexatious litigant.)

In any case, Mr. Baker didn't know the man from Adam, and did absolutely nothing to check out his bona fides.

And Mr. Baker was also in a contest to unseat incumbent Councillor Sandra Bussin, who had supported Mr. Foulidis's proposal and been the alleged recipient of campaign donations from his friends and family. As Mr. Baker put it once, "I was out to get her. I was out to get her removed from office." (As it turns out, Ms. Bussin was defeated, but not by Mr. Baker.)

But he, and the friend who'd forwarded the man's letter to him, nonetheless drafted a letter for Mr. Baker to take to council, which he did in the early afternoon that day.

This letter referred to "new revelations over the [Foulidis] deal," accused Mr. Foulidis of influencing City Hall "for favours," and demanded that council call for both "a full audit" and a Toronto Police investigation.

As Mr. Baker told Gary Caplan, one of Mr. Foulidis's lawyers, "These accusations should have been looked at." He agreed with Mr. Caplan that the allegations were "absolutely" shocking, and that they basically accused Mr. Foulidis of bribery.

But Mr. Baker apparently had no qualms about passing them on to every member of council. He didn't even mark the "open letter" confidential; that nicety occurred at the city clerk's office. There was no recognition that on the flimsiest of accusations, without a moment of checking, he had passed on information about Mr. Foulidis, who learned of the letter only later, that was potentially devastating.

Mr. Baker even tried to cast what he had done as a noble effort to have "the process" examined, to deny that he had been asking for "a criminal investigation" (what was that request for the police about then?) and had the temerity to suggest that though he didn't know

Mr. Foulidis, his brother the lawyer held him in "very high" regard and told him he "was a good guy, and I carried that."

Not long after he sent the letter, Mr. Baker was strolling the beach area, near the infamous restaurant, with his girlfriend when Mr. Foulidis recognized him and began yelling at him.

Others—me among them—would have pounded the daylights out of him.

"I just want a competitive bid": Ford; Mayor doesn't retreat in defamation lawsuit defence

SAT NOV 17 2012
By: Christie Blatchford

An audio tape of the lengthy meeting that is at the heart of the lawsuit Toronto Mayor Rob Ford is now defending makes it clear that he was obsessed with the culture of opacity, untendered contracts and back-room dealing at City Hall—and not with the man he's alleged to have defamed.

That man, restaurant operator George Foulidis, is now suing Mr. Ford, who was then running for mayor, for $6-million for remarks published in the *Toronto Sun* the day after he met the paper's editorial board.

Curiously, and very unusually, the newspaper itself is not being sued, as is the norm.

Mr. Foulidis, 53, runs the Boardwalk Café on a piece

of prime waterfront real estate in the eastern beaches that is owned by the city. The company's corporate name is Tuggs Inc.

In 2010, smack in the midst of the election campaign, the outgoing council refused to reconsider its earlier approval of Mr. Foulidis's new 20-year lease to run the restaurant, with assorted other exclusive rights—including a lock on suntan lotion sales.

The actual contract was inked that summer.

The lease was never put out for tender despite the recommendations—indeed, the strong urging, Mr. Ford testified Friday—of city staff.

Mr. Foulidis alleges he was defamed by Mr. Ford, a very few of whose comments at the board meeting appeared in the next day's paper.

At the urging of the mayor's lawyer, Gavin Tighe, Ontario Superior Court Judge John Macdonald agreed that the entire tape, and a transcript, should be put into evidence to lend context to the disputed remarks.

That is exactly what the whole of the tape does.

The allegedly defamatory remarks in the suit are a reference to "smacks of civic corruption," which the tape reveals Mr. Ford never said and was a paraphrase by the newspaper, and three phrases he has always admitted to saying.

The phrases are "If Tuggs isn't, then I don't know what is" (allegedly a reference to corruption); "It's confidential and I wish you guys knew what happened behind closed doors" and that the deal "stinks to high heaven."

In the same paragraph, Mr. Ford also complained to the *Sun* staffers that "there's more corruption and skull-duggery going on in there [closed-door meetings] than I've ever seen in my life."

Ironically, because Mr. Foulidis's lawyer, Brian Shiller, repeated those words—corruption and skull-duggery—every five minutes and asked Mr. Ford count-less questions about what he had meant or hadn't, the phrase forms no part of the alleged defamation.

In a case like this, which is all about the specific words that are complained of, words matter hugely.

What the tape and transcript show is that the issue of Mr. Foulidis's deal was raised late in the meeting by *Sun* columnist Sue-Ann Levy, who had written exten-sively about it.

Twice she asked Mr. Ford about "the Foulidis con-tract," and only on the second occasion did he reply, "Wha . . . On the Tuggs?"

"Absolutely," he said then. "It's in camera [behind closed doors], it's confidential. I wish that you guys knew what happened in camera, which a lot of you do, obviously, but these in camera meetings, there's more corruption and skullduggery going on in there than I've ever seen in my life. And if Tuggs isn't, I don't know what is. And I can't accuse anyone, or I can't pinpoint it, but why do we have to go in camera on a Tuggs deal?"

Mr. Ford didn't retreat from those words Friday,

but said that by corruption and skullduggery, what he meant was the vote-wheeling and dealing by councillors, a practice he called "horse-trading . . . you scratch my back, and I'll scratch yours. [They] trade votes off, not in an ethical way," he said, meaning councillors sometimes didn't read staff reports, but rather voted in support of a colleague's pet project in exchange for a vote for one of theirs. His real bugaboo—he mentioned it early in the *Sun* meeting—was sole-sourcing—the general practice of not tendering contracts. He raised the subject frequently and cited two contracts—one for subway cars—as examples.

"I just want a competitive bid," Mr. Ford told the *Sun*.

He was in the witness stand most of the day—oddly, because of the way this trial is proceeding, called by Mr. Shiller and thus immediately cross-examined as a so-called adverse witness without the benefit of testifying first in what's called examination-in-chief.

This is allowable under the rules of civil procedure.

Mr. Ford wasn't in the least a hostile witness, however, though he stood his ground—he still believes the Tuggs' lease is a dirty deal simply because it wasn't tendered and because of the links between Mr. Foulidis and Sandra Bussin, who was then the local councillor.

At the time, much was made in the media of about $12,000 in donations that had been made to Ms. Bussin's 2003 and 2006 election campaigns by friends, family and staff of Mr. Foulidis.

Mr. Ford continued to express healthy skepticism that employees making $40,000, who didn't even live in Ms. Bussin's ward, would have coughed up the $750 maximum.

"It's hard enough to get the maximum contribution from your own family sometimes," he said to chuckles from the packed courtroom.

His vivid description of an in-camera meeting where he said Ms. Bussin and other councillors "were going snake, ballistic" over staff's recommendation that the lease be put out for tender also won a laugh.

"In camera," he said at another point, "is sort of an oxymoron: In camera means you're out of the camera. There's no public, no media."

For the man so often painted as Toronto's clown mayor, Robert Bruce Ford had a pretty decent day.

Media a pivotal player in libel suit against Toronto Mayor Rob Ford

Tue Nov 20 2012
By: Christie Blatchford

Again and again, perhaps even dozens of times, lawyer Brian Shiller mentioned the *Toronto Sun* and the allegedly defamatory article in question. He spoke of "sensational" headlines for the purpose of influencing the then-underway election and spoke of his poor client as "roadkill."

Honest to Pete, the mythical "reasonable person" so often referred to in these proceedings, wandering into Ontario Superior Court Judge John Macdonald's courtroom in Toronto Monday, would have been certain it was the oft-cheeky tabloid that was being sued.

But no, the paper isn't part of the lawsuit.

Rather, it is the fellow whose remarks back in August

of 2010 the newspaper brazenly torqued—and in this business, all newspapers do that from time to time, with one newspaper torquing one way and another torquing the other—who is being sued, that is, Toronto Mayor Rob Ford.

Despite a week of by-the-seat-of-your-pants instruction in libel and defamation law that is a byproduct of Ford's trial, I for one still have no clue why or how it is that the alleged roadkill's lawyers aren't also suing the *Sun*, as is the norm.

The purported roadkill is George Foulidis, the operator of the Boardwalk Café, whose corporate name is Tuggs Inc., in Toronto's eastern beach.

He is a handsome 53-year-old who was first awarded an exclusive 20-year lease to build and operate a restaurant on the prime piece of city-owned waterfront parkland.

This was done through a Request for Proposal, an RFP.

As that lease approached its expiry in 2007, Foulidis naturally enough began to try to negotiate for its renewal.

Sadly for him, city staff—on high alert after a recent judicial inquiry into untendered computer lease contracts—decided the city ought to issue another RFP.

Happily for him, city council and various committees ultimately told their own staff to blow that RFP idea out their bums, and gave Foulidis another 20-year lease anyway, with more exclusive rights over more beaches land in what is arguably an even sweeter deal.

At the time that new lease was being finalized and finally signed, Ford was running for mayor and the election campaign was in full swing.

On Aug. 11, he popped into the *Sun* for a meeting with the editorial board.

It was a friendly affair, perhaps akin to the reception a policy wonk would find at an editorial-board meeting at *The Globe and Mail*.

A tape of this meeting was belatedly discovered and is now in evidence at the trial, as is a 30-page transcript. The tape is replete with much chuckling, lots of softball questions, and is brilliant evidence of the old definition of editorial writers as those who come down from the mountain, after the battle is over, to shoot the wounded.

It was only late in the meeting, on Page 22 of the transcript, that *Sun* columnist Sue-Ann Levy raised the issue of what she called "the Foulidis contract." On her second try, Ford replied, "Wha . . . On the Tuggs?"

He then went on to say the three phrases—an apparent reference to the deal being corrupt, that the deal "stinks to high heaven" and that he wished "you guys knew what happened behind closed doors"—that are the alleged libel of Foulidis.

It's the reference to "corruption" that really stung Foulidis, as he testified here last week. He knew the deal was genuinely controversial; there had, two years earlier, even been placard-waving protesters objecting to his lease, and the local councillor, Sandra Bussin, took considerable heat for having gone to bat for the deal.

All of that he could bear, Foulidis essentially said. But to label the deal corrupt was too much to bear, and greatly embarrassed him.

The strange thing about the $6-million suit is that it was the *Sun* that went to town on the corruption angle, not Ford.

The next day, the paper gave over its front page to a picture of Ford (looking remarkably younger than he does now; the bloody job does age the occupant) and the headline, in war-size type, "Council 'corrupt.'"

A subhead read, "Ford lashes out at Boardwalk decision," and inside was the offending story.

Ford's actual remarks about the deal are milquetoast, even circumspect, compared to the play the paper gave the story, though it's certainly clear from the whole tape that he was a strong proponent of tendering and loathed the "horse-trading" that routinely went on at council.

And that infamous meeting, at which council gave the final thumbs up to the deal, was in fact preceded by a three-hour secret meeting, just as Ford had remembered.

His lawyer, Gavin Tighe, will argue that the certified copy of the minutes, showing the break for the confidential meeting, should be considered evidence, and then will complete his closing remarks Tuesday.

Mea culpa: In a column about this last week, because I am a moron, I conflated Ford's testimony about that secret meeting (where councillors, he said, "went snake, ballistic" in fear the deal could be killed and frantically worked the room) with Sandra Bussin's earlier support for the Tuggs' deal and said she was there. In fact, Ms. Bussin recused herself from that entire meeting, the closed-door part included, and didn't vote. She had similarly recused herself from all votes on the deal from February of 2007 on. Apologies for the goof.

Don't blame Ford for spin: lawyer; Decision weeks away as mayor's libel trial ends

WED NOV 21 2012
By: Christie Blatchford

Rob Ford isn't responsible "for the way" the *Toronto Sun* spun or used his words, his lawyer Gavin Tighe said as the Toronto mayor's latest court case closed Tuesday.

Mr. Ford is being sued for $6-million in a libel action by George Foulidis, the owner and operator of the Boardwalk Café, a restaurant in the eastern beaches area of the city.

Mr. Foulidis is also suing Bruce Baker, who two years ago was a candidate for councillor in the ward where the café is located.

Ontario Superior Court Judge John Macdonald, who is sitting without a jury as was the choice of the plaintiff Mr. Foulidis, reserved his decision. It is at least several weeks away as the judge has asked the lawyers for additional submissions and given them time to prepare.

At the time Mr. Foulidis served his notice of libel on Mr. Ford on Sept. 16, 2010, it was near the end of a heated municipal election campaign—Mr. Ford was running for mayor—where the restaurant's controversial untendered lease with the city was a major issue.

The original lease, which Mr. Foulidis won in a Request for Proposal, or RFP, expired in 2007 and had been in various stages of limbo—now approved, then on hold, then approved, then stalled—in the intervening years.

Mr. Foulidis's lawyers, Gary Caplan and Brian Shiller, allege the 53-year-old businessman was defamed as a criminal by both Mr. Ford and Mr. Baker, his lease unfairly painted as corrupt.

Mr. Ford is alleged to have smeared the restaurateur with remarks he made in an editorial-board meeting with the *Toronto Sun* that May, select ones of which the newspaper published in a front-page story the next day.

Mr. Baker is alleged to have similarly tarred Mr. Foulidis by sending city councillors a letter, in which he demanded Toronto Police be called to probe the restaurant deal, hours before council's final vote to approve the exclusive lease.

According to Mr. Caplan, Mr. Baker essentially accused Mr. Foulidis of engaging in a longstanding "practice of bribing city officials"; according to Mr.

Shiller, Mr. Ford "went too far" with his comments and rendered Mr. Foulidis "road kill."

But all that, Mr. Tighe told Judge Macdonald in his closing remarks, is hyperbolic pap.

For one thing, he said, the three comments Mr. Ford is being sued over were but "seasoning" to the newspaper's own agenda to make political hay and sell papers.

Indeed, the paper put the story on the front page over a picture of Mr. Ford and a headline that screamed "Council 'corrupt.'" But the tape of the meeting, and a transcript, show Mr. Ford never said that.

His few remarks about the sweetheart deal, in fact, came late in the meeting, and only after he'd been asked twice about "the Foulidis deal." Of a transcript of 30 pages, Mr. Foulidis is complaining of only 22 words Mr. Ford said, none of which is "corrupt."

As Mr. Tighe put it, "The allegations of criminality flow not from the transcript [of what Mr. Ford actually said] but the article [what the *Sun* made of the remarks] . . . . That doesn't come out of the mouth of Rob Ford," he snapped. "It comes out of the pen of the *Toronto Sun*."

Curiously, and unusually, the newspaper itself is not being sued.

(Mr. Shiller, asked on Tuesday why that was, said he wasn't "ready to talk about that.")

Mr. Foulidis, having chosen to "do business with the City of Toronto," should have been "prepared for the public scrutiny" that comes with the territory, Mr. Tighe said.

Those who deal with public entities ought to know that "part of the package is that they have exposed that business to the sunlight."

Finally, Mr. Tighe said, referring to the millions Mr. Foulidis is seeking from Mr. Ford, "There is not a shred of evidence that Mr. Foulidis is out of pocket one thin dime."

As for Mr. Baker's alleged defamation through his call for a police investigation, Mr. Tighe said, "It didn't hurt [the restaurant] one iota."

After all, he pointed out, the result of Mr. Baker's letter was, "The vote passed and [Mr. Foulidis] got the deal."

That prompted Mr. Shiller to thunder, in reply, that the allegations against Mr. Foulidis were "as serious as it gets, short of calling someone a murderer."

It is always a mug's game to attempt to guess where a judge is heading, and more so in this case, what with Judge Macdonald's even-handed questioning of the lawyers over the past five days, and the little-known (to me anyway) niceties of the civil side of the law.

But a couple of things seem self-evident.

One is that—and there's not a whit of evidence of this—if Mr. Foulidis, as it's alleged he was accused of doing by Mr. Baker, had been bribing city officials, he sure wouldn't have got his money's worth.

The man spent years—almost a decade in total—trying to get City Hall to either re-negotiate his lease, or put it out to tender, or do something.

As his brother Danny told me in a rueful aside, several times Mr. Foulidis was so frustrated by the bureaucracy he was ready to just hand over the keys to the café.

The other thing is, Mr. Foulidis did, in the end, get the deal—exclusive rights to a vast tract of city-owned waterfront parkland, to sell food and booze and suntan lotion and the like—and he got it for 20 years. And that ain't road kill.

Why I once voted for authenticity; Flaws aside, Ford has been the real deal on trial

SAT NOV 24 2012
By: Christie Blatchford

"Is he fun to draw?" I asked an artist friend one day recently in the Rob Ford defamation trial. "He draws himself," she said with a smile.

I knew what exactly she meant—I too have a face that begs for caricature, and my ex could produce with one line a frighteningly recognizable me in five seconds.

But I also thought it was a pretty good metaphor for the Toronto mayor, period: In terms of the various jams he has been in or is in, he drew himself there too. He is so very often the author, and illustrator, of his own misfortune.

I covered Mr. Ford's defamation trial, but not the earlier conflict-of-interest case, which carries the most potentially devastating consequence—he could be removed from office when that decision comes down on Monday.

The two matters have something in common, in that in both cases the allegations sound terribly serious—in the former, Mr. Ford didn't declare a conflict and voted at city council against making himself repay money donated to his football foundation, and in the latter, he purportedly libeled a poor businessman by calling him corrupt.

But in the first instance, the sums at issue are small ($3,150) and there's no suggestion the mayor personally pocketed any of it.

And in the second, the evidence at trial pretty convincingly showed Mr. Ford never uttered the word corrupt, didn't know the businessman, that his obsession was with the deal in question—oh, and that George Foulidis, the maligned businessman, is sitting very pretty indeed with a genuinely controversial untendered 20-year sweetheart lease with the city that gives him exclusive rights to sell food, drink and souvenirs for the vast eastern beach.

In the conflict-of-interest case, the lawyer pushing the complaint forward, representing a citizen reportedly pro bono, was Clay Ruby.

In the $6-million libel trial, Mr. Foulidis had two lawyers representing him—Gary Caplan, who once represented Mr. Foulidis's father in court, and Brian Shiller, one of Mr. Ruby's partners.

This stunning coincidence—that of all the law firms in this lawyer-thick city, two of the three holding Mr. Ford's feet to the fire in the courts are from the same activist firm—was actually addressed by Mr. Shiller in his opening submission.

"Mr. Ford's office has made statements in the press that this case is about politics," he said. "They have gone so far as to suggest that my law firm has some sort of agenda to attack Mayor Ford."

"This case is not about politics, and my firm seeks to represent its client with the sole purpose of putting forward his legitimate claim. Suggestions to the contrary are nothing more than baseless rhetoric."

(Just another reason to adore baseless rhetoric, I suppose.)

Watching the mayor in court was interesting, especially for someone who was, I suspect, one of the few in the room who actually voted for him in the last election.

Almost from the moment I left that polling booth two years ago, I rued it too, from his first fumble with Pride Week (that first year, he'd have nothing to do with it, which I thought ungraceful for a mayor who represents everyone) to a much more recent string of gaffes (calling city staff about fixing the road in front of the Ford family firm, phoning the TTC boss on another occasion) that seemed to show a blockheaded inability to realize that when his own interests are involved he simply can't behave as he would for a constituent.

I've no doubt that if Joe Blow wanted a city road repaired, Mr. Ford would make a few calls. But he seemed not to recognize that he shouldn't come within a country mile of seeking favours if it was for his family company or his football team.

In short, I pretty quickly forgot why I'd ever voted for him.

That week in court refreshed my memory, as the lawyers say. It was never that I loved Mr. Ford, either the detail of his politics or who he is particularly.

Rather, I liked who he wasn't.

He wasn't David Miller, his pretty-boy predecessor. He wasn't the late Jack Layton. He wasn't Sandra Bussin, the former councillor. He wasn't Olivia Chow, another former councillor, Mr. Layton's widow, who may yet return to run for the mayoralty (but only, of course, if "the people" demand it).

Mr. Ford wasn't a part of that soft-left ruling class which, during my time at City Hall in the mid-1990s, ran the show, and appears to still. He wasn't an earnest subscriber to the conventions of downtown city politics, with its sure convictions about What We Believe In.

I remember that so vividly, the smugness, the preening disdain for outsiders, even if, sometimes especially if, they were actual citizens.

As Mr. Ford's lawyer at the libel trial, Gavin Tighe,

said rather forcefully in his closing argument, institutional corruption "isn't done with packets of cash anymore," but through lobbying, campaign donations, the crass horse-trading of votes and backroom deals, and, Mr. Tighe didn't mention this, a collective sort of moral superiority.

Mr. Ford is surely deeply flawed. Well, so are most of us, me anyway. But, to use a modern term, he is also authentic.

Watching him being cross-examined by Messrs. Shiller and Caplan—who once used the word "lacuna" in his closing submission, then, for the rest of us not so smart as he is, added helpfully, "that gap"—was a brilliant reminder of why once upon a time, I marked an "X" by Rob Ford's name.

He's out, but this isn't a case of a corrupt mayor

TUE NOV 27 2012
By: Christie Blatchford

So, Toronto Mayor Rob Ford has been given the boot from office because an opportunistic citizen hired a smart and politically savvy lawyer who found a club of an arcane statute with which to tie the hands of a judge who was willing to play ball.

That's the short and dirty version of the bombshell that has dropped.

There was "absolutely no issue of corruption or pecuniary gain" on Mr. Ford's part, Ontario Superior Court Judge Charles Hackland wrote in a decision released Monday.

In other words, this isn't analogous to the cases involving other Canadian mayors where the allegations are about corruption or the countenancing of corruption—Joe Fontana, of London, Ont., who is facing fraud charges and refuses to step down; Laval's Gilles Vaillancourt, who quit earlier this month after a witness at Quebec's corruption inquiry testified the mayor took kickbacks on all construction contracts; and Montreal's Gerald Tremblay, who resigned Nov. 6 amid accusations he had turned a blind eye to the corruption that was purportedly all around him.

To quote Judge Hackland again: Mayor Ford's case, by comparison, "involved a modest amount of money which he endeavoured to raise for a legitimate charity [his football foundation], which is administered at arm's length through the Community Foundation of Toronto."

Furthermore, as the judge also noted, when Mr. Ford insisted on speaking to the original motion at city council—the integrity commissioner Janet Leiper had suggested council ask him to repay the $3,150 given to the foundation by donors he'd approached using city letterhead—he was trying to clear the air "in circumstances where many informed commentators would contend that the principles of procedural fairness . . . should have allowed him to speak (although not to vote)."

The mayor did, notoriously, vote for a motion that rescinded the order to repay.

As the judge said, his speaking and voting "was far from the most serious breach," but removal is mandatory unless the breach was inadvertent or by reason of an error in judgment.

Mr. Ford's own testimony at trial made it clear it wasn't inadvertent (he said he came to that meeting with the intention of speaking, on principle if you like) or an error in judgment (or that if it was, it was his fault for either not knowing or ignoring the rules). Besides, the judge said, Mr. Ford showed "a stubborn sense of entitlement [concerning his football foundation] and a dismissive and confrontational attitude" to the integrity boss and council's code of conduct.

The mandatory removal required—under Section 10.1 of the Municipal Conflict of Interest Act—makes the statute an ass, as the judge himself acknowledged.

It "is a very blunt instrument and has attracted justified criticism and calls for legislative reform," the judge said.

He quoted no less than David Mullan, a professor in administrative law and Toronto's first integrity commissioner, who six years ago told city council that "it is simply Byzantine to have a regime under which the only way of dealing legally with conflict of interest in a municipal setting is by way of an elector making an application to a judge and where the principal and mandatory penalty . . . is the sledgehammer of an order that the member's office is vacated."

Had Judge Hackland been looking for an out—to address what he pretty plainly agrees is a bad law—his best bet was Section 4(k) of the statute, which says that removal doesn't apply if the pecuniary interest "is so remote or insignificant in its nature that it cannot reasonably be regarded as likely to influence the member."

But the judge found that what the mayor said at that meeting where he shouldn't even have been speaking revealed "his pecuniary interest . . . was of significance to him" and the 4(k) exemption didn't apply.

What Mr. Ford said was this: "And if it wasn't for this foundation, these kids would not have had a chance. And then to ask that I pay it out of my own pocket personally, there is just, there is no sense to this. The money is gone; the money has been spent on football equipment."

(I'd argue that it's just as reasonable to interpret that as the sputtering and clumsy protest of a man who was bewildered how doing something good had turned so bad.)

Thus did the judge join Paul Magder (the citizen who complained) and Clay Ruby (Mr. Magder's lawyer) in using an elephant gun of a statute on a flea of a misdemeanor.

In the post-Charter of Rights and Freedoms world that is the modern Canada, citizens have grown accustomed to taking their laws as much from the courts—the Supreme Court and Superior Courts all across the country—as they do from the Parliament. Indeed, it is often celebrated when the courts overturn laws made by the federal government, especially the Stephen Harper government.

On Oct. 25, 2010, 383,501 Torontonians voted for Rob Ford, 93,669 more than voted for the runner-up, George Smitherman, and just 1,813 fewer than all of those who voted for third-place finisher Joe Pantalone.

Not a one of them voted for Mr. Magder, Mr. Ruby or Judge Hackland.

Jury's out on Ford judge's order

THU NOV 29 2012
By: Christie Blatchford

As lawyers for embattled Toronto Mayor Rob Ford filed their application for a stay of a judge's order giving Mr. Ford the boot from office, the controversy surrounding the order itself is quietly growing.

On Monday, Ontario Superior Court Judge Charles Hackland found Mr. Ford had had "a pecuniary interest" in his football charity when he spoke and voted on the matter at a Feb. 7 city council meeting.

The judge formally declared his seat vacant but allowed a 14-day grace period before the order takes effect.

Alan Lenczner Wednesday filed a motion on behalf of Mr. Ford in Ontario Divisional Court, asking that Judge Hackland's order be delayed until the full appeal is argued.

Mr. Lenczner argues that the case meets the three-pronged legal test for a stay, chiefly that removing Mr. Ford before the appeal is properly argued would do "irreparable harm" to the democratic election which saw him win the mayoralty two years ago by more than 90,000 votes.

"It cannot be right that the democratic process and the democratic will should be denied for a period of another few months while the appeal is being heard and decided," Mr. Lenczner said.

The motion will be argued next week.

Mr. Lenczner said in his factum that Judge Hackland made several critical errors—first when he found that city council had the authority to order Mr. Ford to repay $3,150 in donations to his football foundation; then when he "conflated" provisions under the code of conduct with the Municipal Conflict of Interest Act (MCIA); and finally when he found Mr. Ford had not made an honest error in judgment.

Another Toronto lawyer—he isn't involved in the Ford case—says in a lengthy analysis of the Hackland decision that it appears what Mayor Ford was doing at that council meeting was first and foremost "fighting to defend his reputation . . . He was offended, rightly or wrongly, by what he took to be political attacks on his integrity and the collateral damage on a charity that was and is dear to his heart."

This lawyer, a 30-year veteran, sent me his 17-page

analysis unsolicited. He asked that his name not be used—a prudent move probably, given he is still practising.

What drew his attention, he said, is that as a general rule judges loathe getting embroiled in politics. "Why would a judge jump to effectively reverse the results of an election?"

He has no answer to that, but he found much that was either idiosyncratic or internally inconsistent in the judge's decision.

Among his points:

First of all, Judge Hackland declined to impose any other sanction but vacate the mayor's seat. Under the MCIA, he had the authority to disqualify Mr. Ford from running in further elections. He didn't exercise it. The city's solicitor and others have said they read the decision as prohibiting Mr. Ford from running in a by-election, should it come to that. Nonsense, says this lawyer.

It is surely ironic, the lawyer says, that "when the dust settles, there is no order outstanding anywhere requiring Mr. Ford to repay $3,150 to anyone. Judge Hackland also had the ability to order restitution, but didn't do it."

"In short," the lawyer says, "the financial interest which allegedly justified this train wreck remains unchanged."

His analysis brings a sharp dose of realpolitik to the law. It is relevant, he says, that Mr. Ford, who was a councillor at the time the donations became an issue, was also "to put it mildly a frequent object" of the city's integrity commissioner's attention. He was frequently investigated and "these investigations were generally the result of complaints made by his opponents" who used the commissioner's office to "seek to censure" Mr. Ford. The most famous probe, of course, was, as the lawyer put it, into Mr. Ford's "failing to charge the public for his office expenses."

At the time the issue of the $3,150 in donations first came before council in August of 2010, the city was in the midst of a hot election campaign. Mr. Ford had taken "deliberate aim" at the gravy train driven by his left-leaning colleagues on council. It was against this backdrop the integrity commissioner first found he had breached the city's code of conduct and recommended council require him to repay the money.

But at the Aug. 25, 2010, council meeting, Mr. Ford took part in the debate and voted on the resolution which condemned him. "The matter received significant publicity and occurred in the run-up to a hard fought election." Yet no complaints under the MCIA were received. "The public, in effect, were given the opportunity to judge Councillor Ford's actions in light of the facts which were given full publicity. They endorsed him to a very significant degree."

The MCIA as interpreted by Judge Hackland deems as a potential breach, punishable by mandatory removal, even an attempt to defend oneself at council. "Explaining one's conduct, seeking to justify it, even hiring a lawyer to defend one's conduct before council, all of these actions could result in removal." That is absurd, the lawyer says, and almost certainly contrary to the Charter of Rights and Freedoms and its free expression guarantees.

Judge Hackland made one disturbing finding, the lawyer says. He found in effect that Mr. Ford "lacked remorse" for his original sin—using public letterhead in soliciting funds. "Mr. Ford's disagreement with that conclusion . . . was used as the basis" for the judge finding him guilty.

But, the lawyer says, the MCIA "is not concerned with the code of conduct and whether Mr. Ford is right or wrong in his view of it. He is entitled to disagree—and to disagree vociferously—with political opponents who took a different view of the matter."

In short, the lawyer concludes, the judge had "many options besides the nuclear one," but sought refuge in none of them.

Clinical condition; Does Ford have 'self-defeating personality disorder'?

THU NOV 29 2012
By: Jonathan Kay

The political controversy that brought down Toronto Mayor Rob Ford is abnormal. In a typical scandal, a politician is caught taking kickbacks, using public funds or other assets for personal enrichment, sexually harassing staff or otherwise exploiting his political office in a way that everyone recognizes to be immoral. But that's clearly not the case with Rob Ford: The conflict-of-interest case that brought him down involves above-board donations to a bona fide private foundation that (everyone agrees) truly does benefit children. Even Ford's enemies aren't alleging that he's on the take. Just the opposite: Beginning a decade ago, when he was a city councillor, Ford campaigned to slash office budgets, limousine access and travel junkets. He doesn't have a chauffeur and seems to spend all of his free time (and then some) coaching high school football.

The second thing that's weird about Ford's case is the casual recklessness with which he courted his fate. Read the Ontario court decision in Magder vs. Ford, and you come to understand just how many chances the mayor had to make this problem go away—even after the release of the Aug. 12, 2010 Integrity Commission report that identified his improper use of City of Toronto letterhead to solicit $3,150 in charitable donations from lobbyists and corporate donors.

He could have simply reimbursed the money in 2010, as the Commissioner asked. Failing that, he at least could have acknowledged his obvious conflict of interest—as he was explicitly prodded to do at the time—before voting on a council motion in regard to the Commissioner's recommendations. For someone who is independently wealthy, such as Ford, $3,150 is not a lot of money. Yet even into 2011 and 2012, he wouldn't give up on this petty issue—eventually prodding another city council vote on the issue (this time, with Ford as mayor), in which he once again voted without an acknowledgement of his conflict of interest.

It's almost as if Ford wanted to get thrown out of office—or, if not get thrown out, at least provoke some self-destructive crisis that put his status as mayor in question. This would be in keeping with his other instances of reckless behaviour—including drug use, public intoxication, drinking and driving, and gratuitous acts of rage. In several cases, he compounded the self-destruction by lying about the episodes in easily falsifiable ways.

Many politicians engage in self-destructive behaviour. But Ford is one of the few who persisted with it, shamelessly and without apology, even after he was caught and threatened with legal sanction. And it extended well beyond a few fundraising letters: As this week's court judgment explained, Ford continued to make a practice of distributing his City of Toronto business card to prospective philanthropists he met in the course of city business, and then subsequently hitting them up for donations.

I don't think this boils down to a lack of intelligence. In 2010, he came into the *National Post* for an editorial-board meeting, and I was pleasantly surprised by his speaking ability and lucidity. I also support much of what Ford has done in office—including ending the culture of jobs-for-life that was making Toronto go bankrupt. He and his brother Doug know how to read a balance sheet. They're not idiots.

So then how did this happen? A clue comes from Rob Ford's response to this week's judgment. "This comes down to left-wing politics," he said. "The left-wing wants me out of here and they will do anything in their power to, and I'm going to fight tooth and nail to hold onto my job and if they do for some reason get me out." There is something about Ford's mind, it strikes me, that imagines martyrdom to be the flip side of disgrace—and glory as the flip side to self-destruction.

"Self-defeating personality disorder" has never been included in the Diagnostic and Statistical Manual of Mental Disorders. But it has been proposed as such, and some therapists have identified it as a useful category. Those who suffer from it exhibit a "pervasive pattern of self-defeating behaviour, beginning by early adulthood and present in a variety of contexts. The person . . . chooses people and situations that lead to disappointment, failure, or mistreatment even when better options are clearly available."

I'm no psychologist. And even if I were, I'd be hardpressed to pigeonhole Ford into the myriad masochistic subtypes contained within the self-defeating rubric ("possessive," "self-undoing," "oppressed," etc.). But as a layman, I am convinced not only that Rob Ford is his own worst enemy, but that something in his brain has him programmed that way.

In Ruby's eyes, Ford does no good

FRI NOV 30 2012
By: Christie Blatchford

Though the notion of a "left-wing conspiracy" has a certain appeal, the truth about the people who brought down Toronto Mayor Rob Ford—at least temporarily— is that they are, rather, cut from the earnest, activist, gentle cloth of the committed urban dweller and correct Canadian thinker.

In short, they are the very antithesis of the combative, football-loving, Don Cherry-embracing, plain-spoken mayor from the wilds of Etobicoke.

And the public record shows they share such an affinity for the same sort of causes that they don't need to conspire.

Clay Ruby, of course, was the lawyer who, working pro bono, brought the case to court and got the decision which saw Mr. Ford ordered from office.

Mr. Ruby is a famous Canadian defence lawyer and a bencher with the Law Society of Upper Canada with a long history of taking on activist causes, particularly those with environmental bent (he's a former honorary director of the Sierra Legal Defence Fund and Greenpeace Canada) and free expression (PEN Canada).

His client was Paul Magder, not the furrier of the same name who once fought against Sunday shopping laws, but Paul Magder the certified electronics technologist who works for Iris Power LP in Mississauga.

Mr. Magder, in turn, was drawn into being the face of the case by Adam Chaleff-Freudenthaler, a 28-year-old activist virtually since birth who now works in labour relations for the Association of Management, Administrative and Professional Crown Employees Ontario.

Mr. Chaleff-Freudenthaler went to school with the children of Mr. Magder and his wife Fern Mosoff—Nat and Robin—and according to a recent *Toronto Star* story, it was Mr. Chaleff-Freudenthaler who contacted Mr. Ruby about taking on the case.

Mr. Chaleff-Freudenthaler had already filed his own successful challenge (with a friend named Max Reed) to Mayor Ford's campaign practices in the 2010 election, persuading the city's compliance audit committee in May of last year to order an audit. The results are pending.

In the May, 2011, edition of *Spacing* magazine, Mr. Chaleff-Freudenthaler acknowledged his animus for

Mayor Ford and his policies, but mounted an articulate defence of his motives—the defence of rules, which he and Mr. Reed allege the mayor broke, that keep the financial playing field relatively level for candidates.

Mr. Chaleff-Freudenthaler also took the mayor's brother, Doug Ford, to task after the councillor spotted him at a council meeting and accosted him with a "Hey, you're the guy with the audits" greeting. At some point, Councillor Ford said "What goes around, comes around," at which point Mr. Chaleff-Freudenthaler asked if Mr. Ford was threatening him.

Mr. Chaleff-Freudenthaler said later he felt bullied.

He then brought a complaint to the city's Integrity Commissioner, Janet Leiper, who in the result had Councillor Ford apologize. His apology was deemed unacceptable.

Mr. Magder, meantime, generally keeps a low profile.

At what was essentially a victory press conference at City Hall just hours after the decision came down Monday morning, both he and Mr. Ruby adopted a sober mien.

Mr. Ruby pronounced the result "tragic," tragic that the mayor of such a great city could "bring himself to this."

Standing beside him, the bespectacled Mr. Magder, wearing a sweater vest, called it a "sad day for Torontonians, sad because we've spent so much time and money on this matter instead of nurturing our city and growing it into a wonderful place to live." He pleaded for leaders who would "work together to build a nurturing city."

(Since Mr. Ruby is working for free, and Mr. Ford is paying his own legal costs, it's unclear to what money Mr. Magder was referring. In fact, non-downtowners could be forgiven for not having a clue what Mr. Magder meant, period, but as one who lives in the core, I can assure you this is how such folks speak and they know what they mean.)

Aside from working on a couple of school board campaigns, including Mr. Chaleff-Freudenthaler's in the 2010 election, Mr. Magder has been uninvolved in city politics.

But though he has mostly flown below the radar, he and his wife Ms. Mosoff, who is a federal civil servant with Human Resources Development Canada, are hardly unengaged with civic life.

Through her job, she was a member of ICE, the Intergovernmental Committee for Economic and Labour Force Development in Toronto, a tripartite group funded jointly by the three levels of government whose members meet frequently, sometimes at Metro Hall, to brainstorm.

As a couple, they have signed their fair share of petitions, among them, the Put Food in The Budget petition (which asked Queen's Park to implement a $100 Health Food Supplement for adults on social assistance) and a petition to Support the Campaign for a Responsible

Energy Plan (an initiative of the Ontario Clean Air Alliance, it was against nuclear generating stations).

In 2001, they wrote the Canadian government to express their "grave concern" about the "extreme intellectual property provisions" of a consultation paper on digital copyright issues. They have sent joint emails to city committees.

Ms. Mosoff, who was awarded a Queen's Jubilee medal as a "Caring Canadian," also appears to have signed online petitions on her own, perhaps most controversially, a petition of the Coalition to Oppose the Arms Trade, which sought to stop Canadian Pension Plan investments "in Israeli Apartheid."

In April of 2010, *Toronto Star* food writer Corey Mintz wrote a piece headlined "My dinner with Clayton Ruby."

At it were some of Mr. Mintz's friends, Mr. Ruby and his wife, Ontario Superior Court Judge Harriet Sachs.

Mr. Mintz was doing the cooking. As his friends discussed the "polarizing allegiance to the left or right," Mr. Ruby cut through the verbal red tape, Mr. Mintz wrote.

"I think it's all abstractly meaningless," Mr. Ruby said. "There are people who do good in the world. And there are people who do not. And we make judgments."

And that, I suspect, has much more to do with the efforts to fell Rob Ford than anything else: They do good; Mr. Ford, in their eyes, does not.

Send in Toronto's clowns

SAT DEC 1 2012
By: Rex Murphy

Once presented to the world as a spic-and-span garden of multicultural delights, Toronto now has become
a lurid reality show starring dysfunctional, petty and
self-absorbed politicians—of whom Rob Ford is merely
the most visible and annoying.

Toronto is the city that in 2010 spent a billion dollars hosting a summit meeting of eight people. This
week, it decapitated itself by throwing out a mayor (at
least temporarily) for soliciting about $3,100 using sta-
tionery bearing city letterhead.

Toronto burns money on projects that go nowhere,
painting and erasing bicycle lanes, ripping up rail lines
for useless tramcars, creating and deleting grandiose
public-transit plans.

How has Toronto—by its own fevered account, a
"world-class" city—become a metropolis with no leader?
Red Deer has a mayor. Clarenville has a mayor. But not
Canada's largest city.

Toronto has its fans—Americans who visit for sports and theatre, for instance. But most Canadians commute to this city with reluctance; and some, only if they have to. It is jammed on every major artery, perpetually under construction, the downtown a playground for every marathon, human-rights protest, B-movie production, pop promotion, and sports novelty there is. (Look! It's the "NFL Fan Experience Tour"!) It is as well a cat's cradle of endless by-laws, token greenism and nannyism.

Most tellingly, it is a factory for tribal grudges: the hip versus the hicks, downtown versus the suburbs. Administrations may change, but the clash of factions is continuous, intense and petty.

There are some grand terms floating around to describe the throwing of Ford out the conflict-of-interest window. From one side, it is seen as the "death of democracy"; from another, it is a magnificent illustration of the "rule of law." My view: Please, don't reach for the lexical tuxedo when describing a municipal mud-match. Toppling a mayor is objectively a big deal. But all the fury behind it, the means to get there and the impulses behind the petty coup are as small as only the Toronto city council can make them.

Ford was unacceptable to one faction from the second he was elected. He was Dogpatch. They were Park Avenue. He was grit. They were pearls. They schemed and he bulldozed. If ever there was a politico who gave his enemies a staff to beat him, it was Rob Ford. He drives an Escalade, for heaven sake. The result is now a city without a mayor, and Toronto being smirked at from sea to sea.

Toronto City Hall is the longest-running circus in Canada. The passage from Mel Lastman to Rob Ford—via the interregnum of David Miller, a central-casting elitist with a Prius and a Harvard pedigree—has not been an advance, but more a change of ringmaster.

Will the national embarrassment following this unofficial coup be something of a cure for its excesses? No. Just wait for the now inevitable by-election to choose the next mayor. The whole episode will not really change the character of Toronto's municipal leadership. It will merely have extended and revivified the feuds and factionalism that brought us to this sad point.

A Top 10 in honour of Ford's big day; Clayton Ruby silenced before the media? Shocking

SAT JAN 26 2013
By: Christie Blatchford

With the usual nod to David Letterman, The Top 10 Reasons to Love and Adore and Be Grateful for the Decision in the Rob Ford Case Even if You Don't Love and Adore and Aren't Grateful for Rob Ford:

10. The sight of lawyer Clay Ruby turning his back on a television camera, a feat that previously would have been considered a physical impossibility for the un-shy and, let me be frank, unctuous defender of correct thinking and all proper causes.

But there he was, O be still my beating heart, Friday morning after the Divisional Court decision was publicly released, walking past the CP24 camera and the CP24 reporter yelling questions at him.

I feared the CP24 two would faint away in shock and alarm, but they soldiered on.

9. Blessed silence from the legion of lawyers, chief among them lead vocalist John Mascarin of Aird and Berlis, who for weeks have been flooding the airwaves with their learned opinions that Mayor Ford's argument didn't stand a snowball's chance in hell of succeeding.

It appears their learned opinions were every bit as learned as was the City of Toronto solicitor's, she who, after the original decision, stood to sombrely advise city council that it was her learned opinion that what Judge Charles Hackland surely meant in his original decision was that Ford would not be eligible to run in the next election, whenever that was.

Days later, Hackland had to clarify that he had meant nothing of the sort.

8. The *Toronto Star* did not get to publish Part 2 of FORD'S FALL, as the paper cheerfully called its special, stand-alone, five-page section of Nov. 27, which celebrated Ford's ouster with barely restrained glee.

It was, as it turns out, the newspaper equivalent of the Toronto Maple Leaf fan base, with its penchant for celebrating the playoffs in September.

7. Paul Magder, the formerly famous Spadina Avenue furrier who for years fought Sunday-shopping laws, may have a chance to reclaim his crown as Toronto's best-known Paul Magder from the terminally serious electronics technologist of the same name who was Ruby's client.

At their victory news conference last fall, both Magder and Ruby adopted a Sincere Look, variously lamenting the decision as "tragic" and "sad" for the city, as though they weren't thrilled to pieces and practically blowing up with delight. Magder also said he wanted leaders who would "work together to build a nurturing city."

The real Paul Magder, the furrier, always spoke in plain English, and I say, bring him back to his former position of Magder dominance.

6. The amusing sight of lawyers, who are forever pronouncing upon the wisdom of judges with bootlicking smarminess, revealing themselves to be much like the rest of us normals. Turns out, in other words, they, like most people, love just the judges with whom they agree.

Ruby, for instance, said in a press release Friday that "the court has let Rob Ford off on a technicality." Mascarin told the *Star* that the court was trying to find a way to save Ford's seat. "That is what has happened in this case," he said.

Good heavens, gentlemen: Aren't those the sorts of sour-grapes comments—a "technicality"?—one expects from the non-lawyer rabble?

5. The kids on the Don Bosco Eagles, the high school football team the mayor coaches and loves (and charitable funds for which were at the heart of his conflict-of-interest troubles), lost the Metro Bowl the day after he got the (temporary) boot from office. So now, they too win one.

4. The fabulous juxtaposition of Ruby telling the *Star* on Jan. 24 that an appeal to the Supreme Court of Canada was "a huge long shot," then announcing in his press release, issued before noon on Jan. 25, that he will be seeking leave to do just that.

3. There is one less good reason to consult George Smitherman, one of those Ford soundly defeated in the 2010 election, for comment, about anything.

2. With two of his three legal matters—the third is the pending result of an audit of the mayor's campaign practices—now done, perhaps we will be spared for a time the sight of Mayor Ford attempting to be statesmanlike.

The mayor was clearly aware that the punditry and fellow councillors were clamouring for him to show humility and "reach out" so that "we can all move forward," and all the usual blather (see "nurturing city" above, in No. 7).

Humility, however, is not the strong suit of this scrappy mayor, as was evident in his modest proclamation that his administration was doing "a great job."

Despite describing the entire legal/court experience as "very, very humbling," he wasn't the slightest bit.

Rather, it appeared he had confused the term "statesmanlike" with the phrase "speaking v-e-r-y s-l-o-w-l-y." He spoke as though he were the president of Slow Talkers of Canada, to use a phrase an old friend coined.

What Ford seemed mostly to feel was gratitude, in fact, which was nice. It would have been unbecoming of him to gloat. Mercifully, he left that to others (ahem).

1. See No. 10.

The backstory to Thomson's backside story

SAT MAR 9 2013
By: Christie Blatchford

Long ago and far away, when dinosaurs roamed the earth and I was a young sportswriter, I attended a banquet of some description for some good cause. Seated beside me was a lovely man who was at the time the most famous hockey player in the world.

At some point during the tedious dinner, he squeezed my knee under the table.

As soon as I was able to flee the joint (this was in the years before I knew my tolerance for all such events was absolute zero) and got home, I called my Dad.

"Guess who grabbed my knee under the table?" I cried. "X!"

"Jesus H.!" he said with delight.

It would have been difficult to tell, I'm sure, which of our chests swelled more with pride.

I'm sure to some this speaks to some troubling issues I had, or my father had, or the hockey player had, or just to the bad old days.

That was then.

I thought of it early Friday morning as I began following what my *National Post* and Newstalk 1010 radio colleague, the clever John Moore, immediately dubbed "Assgrabgate," the allegations former mayoral candidate and aspirant Sarah Thomson made against Toronto Mayor Rob Ford.

This is now.

The two attended a swish fundraiser Thursday evening. Shortly after midnight, Ms. Thomson posted comments on her Facebook page, complete with an unflattering shot of the mayor standing beside her, coyly hinting ("Guess where his hand was in this picture? I must go shower" and "Is grabbing someone ass [sic] assault?") that he had sexually assaulted her.

By the time Mr. Moore was on the air for his morning show, Ms. Thomson was being more direct.

The mayor first had made suggestive remarks, she said, "and then he grabbed my ass. . ." She professed herself shocked by the purported behaviour, because it was so out of character for Mr. Ford.

Being a thoroughly modern person, she then went on to immediately diagnose him with a substance-abuse problem, a diagnosis from which she later retreated.

By mid-morning, in a second interview on the station,

this time with Jerry Agar, Ms. Thomson changed some of the details of her story.

Where first she said she had marched herself after the purported incident directly to "the mayor's people"— for political creatures like Ms. Thomson, the phrase has specific meaning, and encompasses Mr. Ford's aides and staff—she now said she had told some "Conservatives" who were connected to the mayor.

(The only people she appears to have named as confidantes were a lobbyist and a Liberal MPP. The latter's office wisely insisted, as though it were 1973, that the MPP was unavailable for comment and simply could not be reached, modern comms notwithstanding.)

Shortly thereafter, a Richmond Hill councillor named Carmine Perrelli, who was at the event, was on Mr. Agar's show.

He said Ms. Thomson casually told his small group that when she had her picture taken with Mr. Ford, he had grabbed her ass. Mr. Perrelli moved on.

Then with a different group, he ran into her again.

She was with a blond friend Mr. Perrelli believes was also named Sarah, and they were plotting how they were going to go back upstairs, where the mayor was still backed into a corner and surrounded by a mob, to set up Mr. Ford by "getting a picture of his hand near [blond] Sarah's backside so she [Ms. Thomson] could use it in the next election."

Mr. Perrelli thought about it for a minute and went

upstairs himself to warn Mr. Ford's handlers. "Where is she?" one asked. Mr. Perrelli pointed to Ms. Thomson, who by then was taking a picture of her friend with the mayor.

Mr. Perrelli intended to say nothing else about it until, on one of the morning news shows, he saw Ms. Thomson, "this woman I had just met the night before telling a story, a story that I knew had other components to it, and they weren't being told."

His version was backed up by Greg Beros, another Richmond Hill councillor.

He was privy only to the second chat. Ms. Thomson was very animated, Mr. Beros said, talking loudly to the other Sarah, and what he heard her say was this: "You know what? We need to go upstairs. We need to get a picture of the mayor's hand near your butt; it would be good for the campaign."

And for the record, neither Mr. Beros nor Mr. Perrelli has a horse in this race; they know neither party.

Mr. Ford has since categorically denied all allegations. His chief of staff has done the same.

This astonishing story with all its twists and turns dominated the local news all the lib long day. Among the most amusing claims was Ms. Thomson's that she wasn't going to take her complaint any further because she just wanted to "get it out there. If we talk about it, we'll change society that way."

(I've confirmed she did mention the purported assault to a pay-duty officer on her way out the door. The officer asked if she wanted to file a complaint; she declined.)

Amid the sea of voices were some fretting that Ms. Thomson was being re-victimized by having the inconsistencies in her story questioned, but when you attempt to try a man in the court of public opinion, you reap what you sow.

There are no rules in that court, no effort at fairness, no publication bans to protect the innocent.

If Ms. Thomson believed she was sexually assaulted, she should have complained to a traditional body with the expertise to conduct a proper investigation, like the police. If she believed the mayor had just been a boor, she should have kept her mouth shut; wherever did the notion of discretion among ostensibly capable adults go?

And if she really wanted to run for mayor again, as she told the Richmond Hill councillors that night, she has done herself in. Torontonians are unlikely to spot any significant difference between Mr. Ford and the woman who would have the job.

As a wise friend put it, "Mr. Train Wreck, meet Ms. Train Wreck."

Media blows to Rob Ford just keep coming; Hounding mayor about rumours inappropriate

Wed Mar 27 2013
By: Christie Blatchford

You want the flavour of the ongoing Rob Ford/*Toronto Star* sideshow, part 735 or whatever it is?

The following exchange ought to do it.

The embattled Toronto mayor was presenting legendary boxer George Chuvalo with an honorary key to the city at City Hall on Tuesday.

This was several hours after the *Star* had landed on doorsteps, as newspapers may do for a while yet.

The main front-page story was about Mr. Ford, with a headline that read, "'Intoxicated' Ford asked to leave gala," and a smaller one said, "Inner circle repeatedly urged mayor to enter rehab."

The gala in question was a military event called the

Toronto Garrison Ball, held Feb. 23. All six who claimed in the *Star* story that Mr. Ford was incoherent or rambling were quoted anonymously; two who saw nothing awry were named; a third, Toronto Councillor Paul Ainslie, said the mayor was asked to leave.

Thus, outside the mayor's office Tuesday, was gathered a huge throng of reporters, TV cameramen and photographers, all of whom went running upstairs, where the presentation was to happen, once Mr. Ford and Mr. Chuvalo emerged to walk the few metres to the elevator. Once at the members' lounge, Mr. Ford made a warm, generous and even funny speech about the 75-year-old former boxer.

The two families, through a Chuvalo son and a Ford brother, are old friends. The mayor said so. He was clearly proud to be paying tribute to Mr. Chuvalo.

After giving an overview of his guest's storied career in the ring, Mr. Ford, without apparent discomfort, spoke of Mr. Chuvalo's enormous personal losses— the deaths of three sons and his first wife, Lynn, were drug-related, suicides or both—and his extensive charity work against substance abuse.

Mr. Chuvalo, looking well and fit, made a gracious speech in return. He appeared shocked at the number of cameras and press there. "I didn't expect this type of response," he said, later adding there were more media present than for his first press conference with Muhammad Ali.

When he finished, a reporter shouted out a question—what I caught was, "Can you talk about leaving the Garrison event?"—about the *Star* story.

Furious, and I suspect embarrassed for his friend, the mayor briefly addressed the allegation, calling it an "outright lie," part of a *Star* campaign against him, and the paper's reporters "pathological liars."

Then he and his press secretary, George Christopoulos, tried gamely to invite questions for Mr. Chuvalo, the guest of honour.

"Any questions for George Chuvalo?" the press secretary asked.

"Mr. Chuvalo," said *Star* reporter David Rider without missing a beat, "you've fought against substance abuse; can you talk about that? And you've also known the Ford family—have you seen any evidence of it?"

Mr. Chuvalo's only concession to advancing years is apparently his hearing; he looked, obviously uncertain, for guidance to Mr. Christopoulos and the mayor.

Mr. Christopoulos asked the reporter to repeat the question.

Astonishingly, Mr. Rider did: "Mr. Chuvalo, you've talked about substance abuse. That's your main focus. There's a story in the *Star* today saying the mayor might have a problem or appears to have a problem with substance abuse.

"Have you seen any evidence of that?"

The question had to be explained quietly to Mr. Chuvalo, who then said he hadn't yet read the paper, and went on to sing Mr. Ford's praises.

It was, in short, not a glorious day for the press. It rarely is when this mayor and the *Star* collide.

I hung around the Hall for a while, spoke to Mr. Christopoulos, who denied absolutely that the mayor had been asked to leave the event as the *Star* reported, and to Deputy Mayor Doug Holyday, who has been around for three mayors. He said the *Star* attention "far exceeds anything" he's seen before.

"No mayor has ever gone through this," he said, wonderingly. "No PM. No politician."

I didn't ask anyone if they thought the mayor has a drinking problem, which may make me a bad reporter. I heard just the other day that the teacher of a friend's college-aged kid had described me in class, rather in passing, as a racist. I have no clue how I'd answer that, or how to demonstrate I wasn't. I think Mr. Ford is in a comparable position.

I regard with scorn the motive, claimed by some of the *Star*'s anonymous sources and inferentially by the paper itself, of wanting to "help" Mr. Ford with his purported problem.

The *Star* story was explosive. One of its authors was Kevin Donovan, one of the finest journalists working in the business. He brought his very good name to the piece; I'm not sure this story deserved it.

But on the larger Rob Ford storyline, the *Star* doesn't have clean hands.

Other of its reporters have not distinguished themselves in their tactics, tailing the mayor to his summer cottage, staking out his backyard at night, being the first to post on its website the spectacularly cruel YouTube footage of Mr. Ford, while on a celebrated and unsuccessful diet, grabbing some Kentucky Fried Chicken.

Mostly, to be perfectly honest, on an ordinary human level, I feel badly for Mr. Ford. If he has an alcohol problem, how dreadful to see it splashed across the front page; if he hasn't, how does he demonstrate it?

At the *Star*, and in other small-L quarters of the city, people were mortified to find Rob Ford won the election. Ever since, as reader Will Newton wrote me Tuesday, "The view is, 'If we can't beat him at the polls, we will keep him so busy defending himself against all manner of accusations (true or not), people will believe the ploys and he will just give up and quit.'

"This sounds too much like the high school I attended, where those who thought they were the elite and the entitled ran the cliques and the rest of us were just trying to get by."

Amen.

THE

SCANDAL

Crack cocaine allegations and the evolving drama of Toronto's Mayor Rob Ford; Neither crook nor cheat, but Ford must go

SAT MAY 18 2013
By: Christie Blatchford

Look Toronto, Mayor Rob Ford is not venal, malevolent or a cheat.

That said, just the sound of his name now makes me want to lie down with a cold cloth on my brow.

It's time for him to go, somewhere, anywhere—his beloved cottage perhaps, for a good long think before he comes out with the cold hard truth, whatever the heck it is.

A leave of absence, if required, would not be out of line, and even his most unpleasant and ambitious opponents on city council and in the press would be forced to play nice about that.

Stepping down, even if only until the next election, to get his personal life in some semblance of order might be best.

But at the very least, if he does nothing else, the mayor has to do a whole lot more than mutter "ridiculous," blame the *Toronto Star* and then vanish into the first long weekend of the summer, as though he were leaving behind nothing more serious than that nasty video of him dashing into a KFC during his much ballyhooed "Cut the Waist" diet.

What Ford faces now is an allegation that sometime during the past six months, while in the company of some lovely drug dealers from Rexdale, he smoked crack cocaine, and that the whole business was captured on what is described as unusually good-quality cellphone video.

The story first broke Thursday night on Gawker, a website whose motto is, "Today's gossip is tomorrow's news."

If that isn't encouraging, the story written by one John Cook is damn interesting.

He got a tip last week from someone looking to sell a video of Ford smoking crack. The tipster provided a tantalizing photo of the mayor with three "young gentlemen," in Cook's clever words, one of whom unfortunately turned up dead in late March, a homicide victim.

Cook travelled to Toronto, met his tipster and in turn the seller, and finally saw the video while in the back of a car parked outside a north Etobicoke housing project.

According to Cook, what it shows is unmistakably Rob Ford, sitting with a clear glass pipe in one hand and a lighter in the other, awkwardly trying to light the pipe. When he finally does, he inhales.

As it turns out, the *Toronto Star* investigative team of Kevin Donovan and Robyn Doolittle also saw what appears to have been the same video, also from the back of a car, on May 3. The reporters saw it three times and concluded it was Ford.

Their report, on Friday's front page, added considerable detail to Cook's.

The men shopping it around are Somali drug dealers.

They want "six figures" for it. The two who claim ownership want to move to Calgary (lucky Calgary). They appear to be simple entrepreneurs.

It is the tipster (this is according to Cook) who seems to want the video out because the mayor needs to be held to account.

The person who actually shot the video claims to be the mayor's dealer.

The video, say the *Star* reporters who saw it, ends with the ringing of a cell; its ring tone is a song, which appeared to startle Ford, whose eyes open a bit. "That phone better not be on," he said.

It is a staggering, astonishing story.

Ford's greatest strength is that he has presented himself as transparent: He is who he is and nothing more.

In the modern jargon, he is deemed "authentic," the guy with whom you could imagine having a beer.

His supporters weren't surprised whenever he was a bit of a doofus. They couldn't have been shocked when he got loud and stupid at a Leafs game (though they might have wondered why the hell he lied about it first) or even to learn he was once charged with a DUI while on vacation in Florida.

He was who he was—a round, pink, self-conscious, shy, sweaty guy, the very antithesis of this city's natural governing class.

Their number is legion, but think lawyer Clay Ruby, former mayor David Miller, Councillor Adam Vaughan and you get the idea.

Ford was always going to be the fat girl schlepping around Holt's in vain, wondering where the big sizes are kept.

He was a figure of scorn from the get-go, even before he won the mayoralty.

Only a Torontonian would understand the classism in this, but it was enough to say, "He's from Etobicoke, for Christ's sakes."

But crack was never part of the deal.

I speak as someone, perhaps the only one person left in Toronto who will still admit it, who voted for him.

He had a noble goal—stop the gravy train, by which I always took to mean the unholy alliance of labour, bloated bureaucracy and political machinery at Toronto City Hall—but in the viper's nest of that place, he could never locate the gravy with precision and couldn't keep up with the train.

He managed a few wins—contracting out garbage service was one—but the sense I always had was of a guy running behind the train as it left the station.

He cannot leave his loyal and decent deputy mayor, Doug Holyday, to handle this ghastly mess, as he did Friday.

He owes his "base," a dreadful word meant to describe his most ardent supporters, a serious explanation—either of how he became the guy with whom they might want to share a crack pipe, or why that isn't so.

Rob Ford: Unfit for office

WED MAY 22 2013

Byline: Jonathan Kay

On May 9—a week before the explosive publication
of allegations about Rob Ford smoking crack cocaine,
along with an associated still shot of the grinning
Toronto mayor allegedly arm-in-arm with figures from
this dark drug-addled milieu—a local Toronto newspaper carried the banner headline "Mayor Spreads
McHappiness." The accompanying picture also showed
a smiling Ford, but this time with a fictional criminal:
the Hamburglar.

It was a classic political photo-op: Ford was on site
at the Eaton Centre in Toronto during the city council's
lunch break, helping McDonald's generate publicity for
their McHappy Day charity fundraising event. It's the
sort of thing that high-profile politicians are expected to
do hundreds of times per year. Indeed, as civic leaders,
it's part of their job.

But that's a job Ford now can't do. Even if the mayor of Toronto retains the confidence of his colleagues at City Hall, his reputation, such as it ever was, is now a joke. If he showed up at a McHappy Day-style event this week, he'd probably be asked to leave by the supervising PR director. No one wants an alleged crack-cocaine user around their party: Even the Hamburglar has his standards. It's not just risk-averse corporate types who will shun Ford. Parents spend their lives trying to persuade their kids to avoid drugs. Would anyone want Ford leading the 2013 Santa Claus parade, throwing out the first pitch at a little league tournament or showing up on the Jumbotron at a football game? His personal brand now has become so toxic that he will be unable to perform the civic functions of his job.

This is especially problematic in a city such as Toronto, where the municipal executive structure gives very little power to the mayor outside of his ability to apply moral suasion on the electorate and on other councillors. Once a Toronto mayor loses the respect of his colleagues, he is more or less finished—because, otherwise, the only thing he has is the one council vote that every other councillor has.

Of course, this is not the first time that Mr. Ford has been made to look the fool during the last 15 years. He has insulted AIDS victims, appeared in public drunk, chased a reporter through City Hall, been arrested for drunk driving, and emitted so many ignorant and vulgar opinions about so many diverse topics that it is difficult to catalogue them. Even before last week's bombshell, I'd argue that Ford already was unfit for the mayor's job. But if the allegations that he's a crack-smoker are true, this scandal would be the worst of the lot.

Crack cocaine is a destructive, horribly addictive drug. Using crack is a serious criminal offence, as is procuring it and selling it. Toronto police officers spend millions of man-hours every year trying to control the drug trade, and sometimes even give their lives in the course of that campaign: It would be a gross insult to their efforts if it were true—as many Torontonians now have come to believe—that their city's leader is waltzing into those same drug dens to mingle with the criminals the police are trying to stop. A person like that cannot and should not be leading Toronto.

It is certainly possible, of course, that none of the allegations are true. The video in question has not been definitively authenticated. The two *Toronto Star* reporters who saw it, and identified the mayor by his distinctive carriage and manner of holding forth, could, theoretically, be mistaken or even (though this seems extremely doubtful) deliberately lying. If so, Mr. Ford should hold a press conference and explain his theory of this grand plot to frame him—alongside, presumably, a libel suit against all the media outlets concerned, and a manhunt for his criminal doppelgänger. If he somehow manages to give a convincing argument—as opposed to just declaring the allegations "ridiculous," which has been his strategy till now—then perhaps he can still limp to the end of this term.

Otherwise, he should resign and seek professional mental-health assistance for his various self-destructive behaviours.

Tick tock: Ford looks to run out clock

WED MAY 22 2013
By: Christie Blatchford

As Don Peat, the *Toronto Sun*'s excellent City Hall bureau chief, asked wryly, "do you suppose he's going to do the football thing and just run out the clock?"

And that, it appears, is what Toronto Mayor Rob Ford is trying to do.

As all around him the storm of serious allegations—that he has been caught on video smoking crack cocaine and consorting with Rexdale drug dealers—continued to whirl, as every late-night show host on the continent has had a go at him, a fifth day passed without any substantive comment from the mayor.

Mr. Ford attended the special city council meeting Tuesday to debate a proposed casino for Toronto; it was a meeting he never wanted. He spoke at length against the notion of such a casino being located downtown; that was an idea he had liked until recently.

Then he slipped out a back door.

His next significant order of business, an executive committee meeting on May 28, is a week away.

The crack cocaine story broke last Thursday on the American gossip site Gawker; the *Toronto Star* matched it, and expanded the tale, the next day.

Gawker's editor, John Cook, and two respected *Star* reporters, Kevin Donovan and Robyn Doolittle, have all seen the video, which was being shopped around for cold, hard cash by the young lads who claim to have sold the mayor crack and then filmed him.

Mr. Ford has twice dismissed the story as "ridiculous" and part of the *Star*'s campaign against him.

In two short scrums on Friday, one outside his home and one outside his office, Mr. Ford essentially repeated the same flat denial: ". . . these allegations are ridiculous, another story with respect to the *Toronto Star* going after me, and that's all I have to say."

Reporters have asked him directly if the video is a fake, and got his broad back in reply.

It is becoming clear that there are only two real possibilities here.

One is that the video is faked, that some techno smarty pants has made a little movie and pasted Rob Ford's head and body over another's or something.

Perhaps such a thing can be done. Someone has set up fake Facebook and Twitter accounts using my name and a publicly available picture from the paper. So it's within the realm of possibility, I suppose.

The other is that the video is legit and that Mr. Ford was indeed smoking crack with the young men.

I haven't seen the video, my connections with Somali drug sellers being just what you might imagine.

But I can tell you how I would react if someone ever claimed to have a video of me doing the same thing—I would be spitting, incoherently mad; I would be screaming my utter innocence from the rooftops, and I could do this and would do it because I know I have never smoked crack or hung around this group.

Therefore, there could be no video of me doing it.

I'm as flawed as the next guy, and there exists the chance that someone could have a picture of me playing golf topless (guilty), or giving an expletive-laden speech after too many drinks (guilty) or dancing on table tops (guilty).

But smoking crack with a bunch of the local yobs from Rexdale? Oh please.

The mayor's supporters appear to accept the notion that somehow, the *Star* either would be involved in such a smear as a faked video or at least a willing dupe in seeing that said smear was spread wide and far.

I can absolutely assure them that this is not what's happened here. No newspaper on earth is sufficiently organized to pull off such a scam. Newspapermen like to uncover conspiracies and write righteously about them; we are far too inept to carry one off.

Secondly, though editorially the *Star* may not be everyone's cup of tea, and though collectively its coverage of the mayor has been obsessive and occasionally puerile, it has mostly been, well, good.

Donovan and Doolittle are serious, proper journalists. The paper is a serious, proper paper. It has serious, proper editors. The very idea that at the *Star*, all these good people would be so blinded by their zeal to get Mr. Ford that they would invent or knowingly perpetrate a fraud is frankly not on the table.

(And again, if the video is a fake, why hasn't Mr. Ford said so? He has missed the several opportunities to do this believably, by the way; were he to later this week or next month denounce the video as a fraud, I'm afraid I will think it's only because he has managed to buy the damn thing himself.)

The mayor's supporters seem to also deeply resent that he isn't benefiting from the presumption of innocence and right to silence that are the hallmarks of our criminal justice system and indeed our democracy.

But Mr. Ford is not a criminal accused. He is not facing the loss of his liberty. He isn't being questioned by the cops in a cell. The vast power of the state is not being brought against him in the form of a criminal complaint.

He is a politician who voluntarily sought the mayoralty and the scrutiny and accountability that go with it. In some measure, he is the state.

The right to silence is a noble one, protected by the Charter of Rights and Freedoms.

But even in the criminal courts, there are some cases where invoking the right, refusing to get in the witness box and answer the allegations against you, tells the jurors all they need to know—that there is no answer.

Even if Ford's on crack, who cares?

FRI MAY 24 2013
By: Jesse Kline

Who says Canadian politics are uninteresting? In the past week, we've witnessed two Tory senators resign from caucus over allegations of improper expense claims, the Prime Minister's chief of staff resigning as part of the same scandal and—juiciest of all—allegations that Toronto Mayor Rob Ford was caught on video smoking crack.

But from my perspective as a (Toronto) taxpayer, the only real scandals are the ones that involve politicians misspending my money. What Rob Ford does on his own time certainly makes for titillating reading, but it doesn't affect his constituents.

It would be one thing if Ford were responsible for laws that keep drugs illegal. But as a municipal politician, he isn't responsible for the Criminal Code. So whatever one thinks of his behaviour, it can't be said to be hypocritical.

Ford is not the first politician to be accused of insobriety. Many of Canada's Founding Fathers likely were drunk out of their minds when producing this nation's legislative architecture. As historian Mark Bourrie wrote in the *Post* recently, "Confederation itself had floated through on waves of free booze." In the U.K., Winston Churchill won the Second World War starting every day with a glass of white wine, instead of tea—and then going downhill from there.

In 1990, the former mayor of Washington, D.C., Marion Barry, was caught smoking crack on video by an FBI sting operation. He spent six months in jail, before being re-elected as mayor. He currently has a seat on city council. Bill Clinton famously admitted to smoking pot, but claimed he never inhaled. Barack Obama also admitted to doing drugs during his college days, something he has never apologized for.

Former U.S. president George W. Bush and current British Prime Minister David Cameron both faced allegations of using cocaine in the past, but went on to have successful careers as conservative politicians. Of course, neither Bush nor Cameron was accused of doing a line while in office, and there certainly wasn't any smoking gun video evidence to support the allegations. But that was the age before cellphone cameras.

The point is that doing drugs does not automatically disqualify someone from holding public office. Were there evidence that Ford was showing up for work high as a kite, that would be a different matter. But right now, we don't even know for sure that the allegations against him are true.

People are mad at Ford not just because they think he did hard drugs: It's also because he was purportedly doing crack in the ghetto with some sketchy drug dealers. That's racist: I highly doubt we'd see the same level of outrage if he was caught doing cocaine with some white bankers on Bay Street.

Crack has a reputation for being a drug used by minorities in poor neighbourhoods, while coke is seen as the substance of choice for rich white people who make a living behind desks. But despite their different reputations, the two drugs are essentially the same thing—although crack is often cut with other substances that potentially make it more dangerous.

Fears about crack use began in the mid-1980s, when the drug began appearing in impoverished neighbourhoods of large American cities. It was commonly thought that crack was more dangerous than cocaine because it led to violent behaviour, was more addictive and caused serious birth defects. The truth is that it's less harmful than originally suspected (though it's certainly addictive and potentially life-destroying, and obviously I wouldn't recommend trying it).

A 2007 report by the U.S. Sentencing Commission

looking into the discrepancy between mandatory minimums for cocaine and crack use found that crack users are more prone to binges, but that it is not more addictive. It also found that "there does not appear to be a neurological difference between cocaine exposed babies and study controls," and that "almost all crack cocaine-related violence . . . occurs within the drug *distribution* process" (my emphasis).

Cocaine is dangerous in any form, and it is a controlled substance, but does that mean that Ford "should surrender his chain of office," as the *Toronto Star*'s editorial board suggests?

Toronto city councillor Ana Bailao pleaded guilty to drunk-driving charges in January—which is arguably more reprehensible than smoking crack because she put other people's lives at risk. She could have hit a minivan and killed a family of six, yet still retains her seat on council. Montreal MP Pablo Rodriguez also admitted to drinking before getting into a car accident in 2010, but was not kicked out of office until voters gave him the boot in the 2011 election. Torontonians knew Ford had been arrested for drunk driving and marijuana possession in 1999, but elected him to office anyway.

My colleague Jonathan Kay argues that the scandal will affect the mayor's ability to get his agenda through council and that he will be shunned by parents and business people, making him unable to do his job as a civic leader. But as any astute observer of Toronto politics knows, council is already so divided that it makes the U.S. Congress look like a model of efficiency.

And while it's true that parents may not want the mayor "leading the 2013 Santa Claus parade," they shouldn't be holding politicians up as role models in the first place. These people are in the business of telling half-truths and deceiving the public—hardly a life that little Johnny should be aspiring to.

Ford comes from a long line of politicians who like to get inebriated once in a while, because politics, like many jobs, is tough. People will always be looking to unwind after a hard day's work—sometimes breaking the law, with a glass of Scotch during prohibition, and a crack pipe in 2013—and politicians are no different.

By focusing on salacious scandals such as possible drug use, we lose sight of what really matters: public policy. There are plenty of ways to attack Mayor Ford based on what he has, and hasn't, done in office. What he does on his own time is not one of them.

Rob Ford will never, ever resign from office

Fri May 24 2013
By: Jonathan Kay

Toronto Mayor Rob Ford inspires loyalty among his followers.

Passionate, stridently expressed, almost cult-like loyalty.

Earlier this week, I published a column making what I thought was a somewhat obvious point: that Toronto shouldn't tolerate a mayor who is a crack-cocaine user. Rob Ford had claimed that a video allegedly showing him getting high on the stuff in a Toronto crack house is "ridiculous," and then avoided any further comment. I argued he would have to do better than that. But not everyone agreed.

"I support Rob Ford. This is a personal matter [and] has no effect on his service as mayor. Who gives a **** if he smoked crack," wrote one. Another told me:

"I [would] rather have a crack head who respects my money than a left-wing pinko wanting my money year after year."

That last one exhibited a prominent theme in the email I got: It doesn't matter what Ford puts in his body—or what kind of example he sets for children. All that matters in life is low taxes—a cause for which Ford is imagined to be a sort of martyr figure. Indeed, some writers suggested that the root cause of Ford's alleged substance abuse is . . . people like me:

"I still admire this guy big-time. He wants to lower taxes for us poor condo and home owners and stop all these stupid spending charges . . . Ford looks tired and [his] eyes [are] swimming: you news hounds jump all over him. You guys keep harassing this poor guy who wants to do a good job. I don't blame him if he were to take drugs (which I doubt, and don't care). [He] may need that to deal with all the unnecessary bad press. It's a form of bullying—big time!"

Rob Ford is a culture warrior, not an ideologue.

In a similar vein, another writer asked me: "Why are you denying that the leftist media is on an anti-Ford witch hunt?"

Putting aside all the other nonsense that is being written by Ford apologists, that last fellow has a point: It is entirely true that much of the media—and especially the *Toronto Star*, which has been aggressively pushing the Ford-crack-pipe allegations (originally reported by

Gawker.com) since last Thursday—has been viciously anti-Ford for years.

Back in 2010, it must be conceded, the *Star* was entirely correct to warn us about Ford's status as a late-night-comedy municipal embarrassment on two legs. But their journalistic tactics were so over the top that they actually pushed many Torontonians into the Ford camp—especially when *Star* columnist Bob Hepburn wrote a series of bizarre and desperate-seeming columns purporting to instruct marginal contenders to drop out of the 2010 mayoral race in order to firm up the anti-Ford vote behind George Smitherman.

Even worse was when a *Star* reporter skulked around the periphery of Ford's house, ostensibly to report on a real-estate transaction involving a neighbouring property. When Ford confronted the reporter, the *Star* reported on the event on its own front page as if JFK had just been shot—complete with Dealey Plaza-style maps of Ford's home and every footstep taken by their intrepid reporter.

That was a low point for the *Star*, one of many they've hit during the course of a campaign against Ford whose obsessive quality sometimes has appeared to verge into the domain of mental infirmity. And that's a shame, because the *Star*'s alleged-crack pipe story is a legitimate investigative bombshell—as will be the various follow-up stories that the *Star* will print now that other underworld characters will beat a path to the newspaper's reporting staff.

For this diminished credibility, the *Star* has only itself to blame: It is the newspaper that cried Ford.

The *Star*'s obsessive vendetta against Ford also helps explain why Ford hasn't stepped down yet—and, in my opinion, never will.

Like his fans, Ford correctly sees himself in an existential struggle against left-wing Toronto snobs who always have hated everything about him—not just his policies, but also his coarse habits and the company he keeps. And a man in that sort of struggle is never going to give his enemies the pleasure of uncontested victory. Such struggles bring out the tribalistic mettle in people: They fight to the end.

Many people speak of Ford as a "conservative"—as if we were dealing with the Canadian equivalent of a Tea Party leader being hounded by the IRS. But that's not it at all: Ford vacations in Cuba and has promoted spending billions on new subway lines. He doesn't read the Weekly Standard or the policy papers from Fraser Institute. His "conservatism," such as it is, is a spasm of suburban populism operating in righteous fury against the fashionable urbanism of annoying *Toronto Star* darlings such as David Miller and Olivia Chow. He is a culture warrior, not an ideologue.

In the spirit of all true warriors, he will keep on fighting till the very day—if it ever comes—that he is led out of City Hall in handcuffs.

And even then, I'm not so sure.

Canadian journalists have moved the goalposts in pursuit of alleged Rob Ford crack scandal

SAT MAY 25 2013
By: Christie Blatchford

So distressing do I find the Rob Ford spectacle that covering a terrible murder trial in Ottawa, as I did for a couple of days this week and last, came almost as a reprieve, a step out of the gutter.

It is diminishing even to watch the daily unfolding of the story, the latest installment of which late Friday saw the Toronto mayor belatedly deny that he uses or is addicted to crack cocaine.

As for the cellphone video at the bloody heart of the whole business, Mr. Ford said merely, "I can't comment on a video that I've never seen or does not exist."

In this at least, the mayor isn't alone.

At this writing, aside from the Rexdale drug dealers who are reportedly shopping about the video of Mr. Ford allegedly smoking crack and grunting disgraceful slurs, only three people—an editor with the U.S. gossip site Gawker and two reporters at the *Toronto Star*—can even claim to have seen it.

Yet here I am, having another go at the subject. I do it for two reasons.

The first was illustrated by Toronto's deputy mayor, Doug Holyday, who came before the press pack at City Hall before the mayor did and pulled off the impossible—he managed to address the issue in a straightforward manner, but the compassion he felt for Rob Ford the man was palpable.

Mr. Holyday did all the right things.

He urged the mayor to address the public, and to judge by Mr. Ford's thanks a few hours later, his opinion carried some real weight.

Mr. Holyday reassured the public, not that the public ought to have needed it because bureaucracies are after all self-sustaining, that things are still running tickety-boo. Water still comes out of the tap; you can still check out a book at the library; police and fire are still on the job and, oh yes, council has met this week (to kibosh the casino) and so has the executive committee.

He refused to get in the muck. He wouldn't call the situation a crisis. He wouldn't play pop psychologist, saying only, "If he [the mayor] has problems, he should do something about it."

But mostly, in his evident concern for Mr. Ford's welfare—"I just think it's a lot of pressure on him"—Mr. Holyday injected a note of kindness that has been almost entirely absent, eight days into the saga.

He is such an adult, and such a decent, nice one.

Whatever else, the city has been witnessing the destruction—self-destruction, if you prefer—of a fellow human being.

It ought not to be a joyous occasion, whatever your politics, to watch a man being humiliated in public, dogged by reporters at every turn, and lose the thing that seemed to matter to him as much as anything else in the world, and to bring him joy—his volunteer job as the coach of the Don Bosco football team.

Neither should it be a source of glee, and gleeful does describe the Gawker crowdfunding efforts (at $145,000 as of 5 p.m. Friday) to raise $200,000 for the entrepreneurial drugsters.

But the thing that is troubling to me, and which has gone largely unnoticed or unremarked-upon, is how the ground has shifted in the practice of journalism in this country.

This coalesced in my head mid-week, when I got a smart email from a reader in Quebec named Charles Bogue, and who has given me the green light to quote from it.

Mr. Bogue wrote after I had last typed on this topic, defending both the *Star* and in particular its fine reporters, Kevin Donovan and Robyn Doolittle, who saw the video in question. Mr. Bogue was heartened by what I'd written, he said, though still retained a concern about the story.

"My understanding," he wrote, "is that one of the most fundamental rules of good journalism is to always—always—obtain a corroborating source for any material allegation before a story is published.

"Furthermore, when someone's personal reputation is at stake, simple human decency if not journalistic professionalism, ought to dictate particular care in sourcing any allegations, since informants may have many and diverse motives other than a pristine dedication to the truth for feeding a juicy story to a journalist.

"The *Star* has very conspicuously run, without any form of corroboration, a story it obtained from a couple of professional criminals, and unless I am missing something, I find it appalling that such a practice can be passed off as good journalism."

Mr. Bogue is correct about much and maybe all of that, I think.

Traditional practice is that reporters do seek corroborating sources (the corroboration here, I suppose, came from the reputable reporters who watched the video, three times, from the back seat of a parked car) and certainly in years past, Canadian newspapers are unlikely to have gone to town on the say-so of people as dubious as drug dealers.

As Mr. Bogue points out, these folks "have an obvious motive for concocting a real whopper, to wit: The market value of a video that purportedly shows Rob Ford smoking crack will be considerably higher than that of a video showing him smoking some less noxious substance; and the market value of a video determined to be fraudulent will be zero.

"The *Star* is acting a bit like the person who buys 'an authentic Rolex' from some guy who sells it out of the trunk of his car for $500.

"'Nice chap; didn't quite catch his name, but he assured me himself that the watch is authentic.'"

Add to that a couple of other facts: Gawker said this week it has lost contact with the video seller, who has apparently gone to ground, and in an interview Thursday with 680 News, Mr. Donovan also said his paper is "certainly considering" buying the video, though he called the asking price "outlandish." Not paying for stories has heretofore been a badge of pride for Canadian journalists.

It's inarguable, I think, that with this story, the goalposts of the newspaper business in this country have been moved. They won't be moved backwards.

Toronto unified in name only; Culture war between Ford fans, urban elites

TUE MAY 28 2013
By: Jonathan Kay

As a Montreal native, who grew up amid the language wars of 1970s- and 1980s-era Quebec, the hysterical tenor of Toronto municipal politics is somewhat shocking to me: the hate-on between Mayor Rob Ford's suburban supporters and the downtown folk who mock and loathe him may be just as intense and vicious as the expressions of anglo-franco antipathy I once observed in Quebec's largest city.

And as in Montreal, Toronto's conflict is rooted in history.

I was reminded of this a few days ago, when I was attending a school fundraising fair in my Toronto neighbourhood.

At one of the tables, where volunteers were selling used toys, sat a board game I vaguely remembered from the early 1990s: Toronto Venture Challenge. It's loosely modelled on monopoly, with squares marked "The Danforth," "The Annex," "Little Italy," and so forth. The object is to establish the most "businesses and attractions for residents and tourists of Toronto."

It's a fine example of Mulroney-Era Toronto kitsch.

Indeed, I have never seen a crisper summary of Toronto's boastfully insecure self-image than the promotional blurb that appears on the 1994 game box: "Capture the thrills of Toronto . . . Toronto's excitement and mystique comes alive in this fast-paced, fun for the whole family board game. Residents of this world-class, cosmopolitan city and visitors from around the world alike, admire and amaze at the exceptional attractions, family entertainment and the cultural surroundings."

The idea that the Toronto of two decades ago had a "mystique" worth capturing in a board game is amusing—as is the notion that anyone might have considered a June Rowlands-era Toronto to be any more "world-class" than, say, Cleveland or Denver. Yet the blurb perfectly captures the tone of striving and ambition. I've lived in a dozen different cities, but never one whose elites more openly agonized about their city's international status than Toronto's did in the 1980s and 1990s.

But give those Toronto elites their due: They eventually prevailed. Twenty years ago, *The New York Times* or the BBC might have identified Toronto as "a large city in the Canadian province of Ontario." These days, it is, much like "Los Angeles" or "Berlin," just "Toronto"—a world-class (yes, I will use that term) hub for arts, money, architecture and high-value immigrants.

In this way, Toronto is like that insufferable kid you went to high school with—the one on student council who dressed in a suit and told everyone how rich and successful he was going to be. And then you meet him on the street when you're both in your 40s and, doggone it, he's got the Rolex and the corner office. You hate to admit it—especially since he still talks way too much about himself—but the insufferable dweeb made good on his old boasts.

This is why Toronto, which still maintains vestiges of its old insecurities, gets into such a tizzy about anything that might embarrass the city on "the world stage": Like all parvenus, we Torontonians are mortified that someone might pronounce us a fraud, and undo all our years of social climbing.

The city's elites are scandalized by Rob Ford not just because they don't like his policies (which actually have been a success in many cases), but because his self-destructive buffoonery threatens to undo Toronto's hard-earned "mystique." The Toronto of urban gurus Richard Florida and Jane Jacobs is supposed to be a nirvana of bike-riding graphic artists, not lumbering hotheads ripe for any manner of 12-step programs.

But the people who populate Rob Ford's base—broadly known as "Ford Nation"—don't care about la-di-da urban planners. Most of Ford Nation lives in communities that, until amalgamation in 1998, weren't even part of Toronto. What they care about is waste collection, traffic and low taxes. And they resent the idea of their municipal government being captured by people who put hubris before highways, board games before balance sheets.

This is an intra-municipal culture conflict that will go on long after Rob Ford leaves office. The late-90s amalgamation made Toronto a unified entity in name only. Scratch the surface, and you find two very different political tribes locked together in the same city.

No easy rules; Media never have certainty with any story. It's always a gut call

SAT JUN 1 2013
By: Andrew Coyne

It's been a good few weeks for us media maggots. Some great work by reporters at CTV, CBC, the *Toronto Star* and *The Globe and Mail* has broken a number of big stories that have dominated political debate. The past week also brought reminders of the *National Post*'s original reporting of Arthur Porter's questionable business activities, as well as the painstaking unravelling of the robo-calls scandal by Postmedia's Steve Maher and Glen McGregor, triumphantly vindicated by last week's Federal Court ruling.

Nonetheless, much of the reporting has raised eyebrows, not to say qualms—in the industry and out—pushing boundaries that might not have been pushed in the past. The *Star*'s decision (hard on the heels of the Gawker website) to report on a video of the mayor of Toronto, Rob Ford, purportedly smoking a crack pipe, was dismissed in many quarters, since the paper was unable or unwilling to obtain the video itself, but relied on reporters' accounts of it.

The *Globe*'s reporting on Doug Ford, the mayor's brother, and his alleged involvement in the drug trade as a young man was also widely criticized, not only for being based almost exclusively on unnamed sources, but on grounds of relevance: Was it really in the public interest to poke about in what he might or might not have done 30 years ago, long before he was in public life? Doug Ford's vehement denials of the allegations relied heavily on both criticisms.

The stories, in short, raise two age-old questions: 1. What do we know? How much certainty does a paper need before going to press with a story, and how much weight should readers attach to it? And 2. What should we know? Where and when is it justified for the press to report on the private behaviour of public figures, now or in the past?

I happen to believe both stories passed these tests, both of reliability and relevance. But I can't imagine it was an easy decision for either paper, and second-guessing them shouldn't be any easier.

There is no bright-line rule, that is, to which one can refer. You never have perfect certainty with any story: It's always, at some level, a gut call. Nor is the line between private and public so hard and fast as some would have it.

Let's take the second point first. Often people will assert that a public figure's private life is never relevant. Even the payment of $90,000 to Mike Duffy by the prime minister's chief of staff was ruled off limits by some critics: "What Nigel Wright does with his own money is his business." The absurdity of the claim—a payment by one serving public official to another is hardly a private matter—should suggest it's a little more complicated than that.

Certainly we should not fall to the other extreme, that everything is fair game. The test, it seems to me, is whether the behaviour is something a fair-minded reader would find relevant in assessing a person's fitness for public office. Again, there's no rule book we can consult for this: It requires the exercise of judgment. But that judgment can be informed by certain principles.

If, for example, the behaviour is so common as to be trivial—if a politician drank as a teenager, say, or had premarital sex—everyone recognizes it's not worth reporting: though even here, standards change over time. Once, it might have been considered newsworthy that a politician was homosexual. Nowadays it would, rightfully, bring scorn down on any paper that published it. We seem to be arriving at the same understanding with regard to pot use, at least as a "youthful indiscretion."

But the allegations were not that Doug Ford used drugs, but that he dealt them: indeed, that he was a fairly major supplier of hashish, the dealer to other dealers, and not briefly, but for some years. This raises a number of questions: Who, in that alleged scenario, would his suppliers have been? Can you really just cut off all ties with those sorts of people? And wouldn't a history of family involvement in the drug trade be relevant to the mayor's alleged drug use?

So no, I don't think we can shrug, "it's his private life," or "it was long ago." If the alleged misdeed is serious enough, it may indeed be relevant. Where the matter is in doubt, in my view it is best to publish, and trust the judgment of the people. There's a tendency to see the question in stark, binary terms, as if the mere reporting of some private matter meant automatic disqualification from public life. But time and again the public disproves that. The American people knew Bill Clinton cheated on his wife: they elected him anyway, twice. (That doesn't necessarily mean they found it irrelevant: only that it wasn't the only consideration that informed their vote.)

But even if relevant, were the stories reliable? Can we believe a story based on anonymous sources or unverified videos? Honest skepticism is certainly in order. But there's a point at which an obstinate refusal to draw reasonable inferences from the evidence—to exercise judgment—crosses over from skepticism into denial.

We are not dealing with some rumour on an Internet comment board here. The *Globe* story cited 10 different sources; it was run through layers of editors, and lawyers after them. The *Star*'s reporters watched the video themselves: Their reports were based on first-hand observation, the same as if they had witnessed a fire. So to discount their story, you have to believe that they are making it up, or that they were mistaken about the identity of the man in the video, or that the video was faked. (The last is most often claimed: people who know the technology insist it is not possible, and a moment's consideration of the difficulties involved would suggest they are right.)

That doesn't prove either story is true. It does suggest we should not simply dismiss them out of hand. The allegations are so serious that both papers would have to have known they were betting their reputations, and heavy financial losses, if they were found to be in error. Is it plausible they would do so without having substantial grounds to believe they were true—not absolute certainty, perhaps, but something near to it? Put it this way: Which requires the more elaborate and unlikely set of conditions to hold—that the stories are true, or that they are false?

Everyone is entitled to the benefit of the doubt. But the presumption of innocence does not require us to believe in fairy tales.

Police force in a delicate position; To confirm or deny Ford probe creates conflict

FRI JUN 14 2013
By: Christie Blatchford

When Toronto Mayor Rob Ford's name first surfaced on wiretaps in a lengthy guns-and-drugs investigation, the senior command at police headquarters had to figure out how on earth they would handle it.

Toronto Police Chief Bill Blair's line in the sand was a simple, "I won't lie."

Postmedia has confirmed that Mr. Ford's name came up in some of those wiretapped conversations, though the context isn't clear.

This was, a *Post* source said Thursday confirming a CTV report, before the gossip site Gawker and the *Toronto Star* first reported almost a month ago that drug dealers were shopping around a cellphone video allegedly showing the mayor smoking crack cocaine.

The mention of Mr. Ford's name was tangential to the massive and expensive probe now known as Project Traveller.

After all, the targets of that year-long investigation who were rounded up Thursday in early-morning raids in various locations in Toronto (including apartments in the same Etobicoke complex on Dixon Road which has been identified in the media as the likely location where the alleged Ford video was shot), Windsor and Edmonton.

They are allegedly big-time criminals—drug and arms dealers and those suspected of crimes as serious as murder and attempted murder—belonging to a gang called the Dixon City Bloods.

Police believe their impact went far beyond that narrow slice of turf, though they also believe the gang's local influence was enormous, and that the many good people in the complex in particular lived in fear because of them.

As Chief Blair and Deputy Chief Mark Saunders told reporters Thursday at a press conference, the raids yielded an initial haul of 40 guns, $3-million in narcotics and $572,000 in cash.

Nineteen people were arrested in Toronto, another nine in Windsor. Fifteen others were arrested earlier in the investigation, which began in June last year.

It's also worth noting that merely being mentioned, or the alleged video being mentioned, in a wiretapped conversation doesn't constitute evidence of wrongdoing against Mr. Ford.

Project Traveller had genuinely bigger fish to fry when the mayor's name popped up, like a bad smell, smack in the middle of it.

But its mention was nonetheless immediately recognized at police headquarters as potentially explosive.

Therein lies the bottom line of the delicate dance in which the Chief and the force have been engaged ever since.

To confirm the force was investigating a link to the mayor would give credibility to the questions reporters were asking the police almost daily.

To deny it might appear the force was giving the mayor a pass.

Thus the line that became the force's mantra for the past three weeks plus: Whenever the Chief or force spokesmen were asked about the mayor, the answer was that the police were "monitoring the situation"—an almost deliciously non-committal response that added fuel to neither version.

The line had the added benefit of being true: Mr. Ford wasn't and isn't under investigation.

At the Thursday press conference, it was deja vu all over again.

Of about 30 questions from a room full of reporters chomping at the bit, only a couple weren't directly about the mayor and his alleged links to Project Traveller.

Chief Blair steadfastly refused to be drawn into that discussion, repeating until he was pink in the face that ". . . all of that evidence will be made public in the proper forum—and that is a court of law," that "it will come out in court . . . there's a right way and a right place" and that "All of the evidence gathered in this case is appropriately disclosed at trial."

It wasn't the police chief who ought to have been fielding all those questions about Mr. Ford, but rather the elusive mayor himself.

Chief Blair was directly asked several times why, if the mayor wasn't linked in any way to the investigation, he couldn't just say so. He just didn't.

There was that line in the sand.

Police work and the public interest; Ford questions overshadow fight against gang violence

SAT JUN 15 2013
By: Christie Blatchford

Among the questions that Toronto Police Chief Bill Blair answered the other day, this at a press conference held to discuss a major guns-and-drugs investigation called Project Traveller but which predictably became a session about Mayor Rob Ford and his alleged links to dubious characters within the project, were a handful with a single theme.

By my recollection, and I paraphrase here, the first was, "If the mayor is caught up in a major investigation, doesn't the public have a right to know?"

The second, more of a statement, was, "But there's enormous public interest around this particular set of circumstances?"

The third was, "Doesn't the public interest outweigh other concerns?"

(There was another, and it was the funniest. It came after the Chief had deftly answered the first inquiry by saying all the evidence would come out in court, and from deep within the scrum behind me, somebody cried, "Why can't you just tell us now!" In my imagination, I heard the petulant stomping of a tiny foot.)

The questions bring into focus a couple of things.

The first is that, in my business, we journalists always assume that we are the repositories of the holy trust that is "the public interest."

In fairness, journalists and our newspapers or networks, the organizations that pay for the media lawyers who fight these battles, often do the work that other citizens can't.

We, or our lawyers, argue and rail against publication bans, file the paperwork and/or do the necessary bootlicking to get access to court records and government documents, and claim as sacred duty what was once famously described by one of our own, the American newspaperman Finley Peter Dunne, as comforting the afflicted and afflicting the comfortable.

So we do genuinely often represent the public interest, though it should never be understood to mean that we aren't also simultaneously acting, or capable of acting, in our own.

That brings me to the notorious video watched by two excellent *Toronto Star* reporters, Kevin Donovan and Robyn Doolittle, which allegedly shows Mayor Ford smoking crack.

For the record, I don't doubt the video exists; I know those reporters and they didn't dream this up.

But I haven't seen it and I am desperate to do so, though not perhaps as desperate as the folks at the *Star*.

The paper's original story about the video appeared on May 16. (The first report of it appeared on the U.S. gossip website Gawker hours before, which seems to have pushed the *Star* to print.)

Despite frantic efforts, the video appears to have fallen off the face of the earth. The middleman who was shopping it around town to media outlets has apparently lost contact with the Somali drug dealers who had it. And in the 31 days since the story broke, it hasn't surfaced.

In the interim, various press reports have connected Mr. Ford to some of the lovelies involved in Project Traveller and to the Dixon Road apartments that were its focus and are home turf for the Dixon City Bloods gang.

In a picture that was given, in classic drug dealer fashion, to Gawker and the *Star* as a "taste" of the goods, the mayor posed in front of a home that is an alleged crack house with an arm around one young man (Anthony Smith) who became a homicide victim and beside another (Muhammad Khattak) who was arrested in this week's raids.

Thus was the stage set for the Project Traveller press conference Thursday.

Chief Blair was pressed to say something—anything— about Mr. Ford's alleged connections to the project, and refused. Neither did he take the opportunity to distance the mayor from the investigation.

As I reported Friday, Mr. Ford's name did come up on investigation wiretaps. So while Chief Blair was as discreet as he had to be—it isn't evidence of wrongdoing to be mentioned on a wiretap, for which we should all be grateful—he also had his own personal line in the sand and wasn't going to lie.

There is little doubt that there is a legitimate public interest in knowing how Mr. Ford's name came up on the wires and what is, or isn't, his connection to all of this.

How well or not we in the press represent that interest, on this lone occasion, I'm not nearly as sure about.

Is it just reporters who want to see the damn video? Are readers and viewers as obsessed (Friday, the *Star* devoted its entire front page and six full pages inside the paper to the story, as well as its lead editorial) as we are?

And even if they are as keen as we are, surely no one believes that the public interest always equates to what the public is interested in knowing or watching.

This truth was represented nicely at another police conference, held Friday at 23 Division, where a double-length buffet table of firearms, and a half-million in cash, seized in the raids the day before, were on display.

This division for years has had the most shootings and "sound of gunshot" reports in the city, its veteran boss, Superintendent Ron Taverner says. Yet people in the Dixon Road complex had become so overwhelmed by the gang violence that often they didn't even bother phoning 9-1-1.

Deputy Chief Peter Sloly, who has served overseas, compared it to a soldier's first few days in a war zone: The first night, you sleep with all your gear on, weapon at hand, and barely nod off; the second, the weapon may be close, but you sleep; by the third, you don't even hear the gunfire.

There's a lovely park between the Dixon Road towers where few people, except gang members, dare go. It's that reclamation of public space, civic engagement, that deputy Sloly wants to see happen as the police try to build resilience in the community.

Not long ago, in one of those buildings, the body of a homicide victim lay in a common hallway for more than 10 hours.

For all that time, residents stepped over and around it, too afraid even to report that someone had been killed. Supt. Taverner confirmed "that's what we believe happened."

Fixing that, making Dixon Road safer, now that's also in the public interest.

Happy, polite gangsters appear in court; Two were in notorious Rob Ford video

Thu Aug 8 2013
By: Christie Blatchford

For a purportedly disreputable group of alleged drug-and-gun gangsters, you never saw such a pleasant, cheerful and well-mannered crew as the Dixon City Bloods.

Most of the accused members of the now-notorious gang, alleged to be a criminal organization, made brief appearances Wednesday at the Finch Avenue West courts in Toronto.

The majority were arrested in June in raids that were the finale of the year-long Toronto Police investigation called Project Traveller.

Among those appearing in court were Monir Kassim and Muhammad Khattak, two of the men in an infamous photograph with Toronto Mayor Rob Ford outside an alleged drug den (a third man in the picture, Anthony Smith, was subsequently shot to death, while Khattak was injured), and Mohamed Siad, one of two other men who allegedly showed and tried to sell two *Toronto Star* reporters a video showing the mayor smoking crack cocaine.

These three, like virtually all the alleged gang members who came before Justice of the Peace James Clare, were so exquisitely polite that it sometimes seemed everyone was in on a secret plan to act out the ancient Alphonse and Gaston comic strip, where Gaston famously said, "After you, Alphonse," and Alphonse replied, "No, you first, my dear Gaston."

In one typical exchange, one young man who is accused of participating in the Bloods for the purpose of enhancing the gang's ability to traffic in weapons and drugs, appeared by video link from a local detention centre.

A date set for his next appearance, and with a winning smile on his face, the young man thanked the justice of the peace and said, "Have a good day, sir."

"Thank you," said Clare, not to be outdone.

In another exchange, the justice of the peace was explaining to Ahmed Farah that they were having technical problems with the video link, and that though he would be speaking to a blank screen, the J. P. and court officials could hear and see him.

Farah at that moment was alone on the screen.

But in the next, three of his co-accused—who also had video appearances to make—were beside him.

"You got a poker game going on there, sir?" Clare asked, which made Farah laugh.

On and on for several hours it went like this, with most appearances lasting only a few minutes and virtually all of them conducted with the utmost courtesy.

About 25 people in Toronto and Windsor were arrested in the June 13 raids, with others arrested earlier in the probe, and a couple picked up since.

Given the length of the investigation, disclosure to defence lawyers is far from complete, but is apparently moving along, with the lawyers Wednesday receiving seven DVDs of information and a 32-page index.

Most of those charged will be back in court—a "global remand date" it's called—on Oct. 1.

Should have aired his dirty laundry; Scandal could have been over months ago

Fri Nov 1 2013
By: Jonathan Kay

What goes on in the brain of Rob Ford? On Thursday morning, the Toronto mayor emerged from his house, knowing full well his driveway was mobbed with reporters. That Ford would stumble aggressively across his property yelling at these journalists was no surprise—we've seen variations of this spectacle many times since he took office in 2010. What was weird, in this case, is that the mayor chose to confront these journos with what looked like a wad of clothing destined for the dry cleaner balled up in his right hand.

Put aside the obvious metaphorical significance of a man literally airing his dirty laundry in public: Why is the mayor of Toronto doing his own dry-cleaning chores? Doesn't he have helpers for this sort of thing?

Helpers such as, say, Alexander "Sandro" Lisi, a fellow who seemed especially open-minded when it came to assisting His Worship. According to police documents released on Thursday, Lisi worked his phone for hours after media reports in May first disclosed the existence of a video showing Ford inhaling on what appears to be a crack pipe, dialing up a who's who of Toronto drug-world figures in one marathon all-nighter session.

In a single 44-day period that followed, the police determined, Ford spoke with Lisi—an accused drug dealer and blackmail artist who's been convicted for threatening and assaulting women—a total of 349 times. Ford and Lisi also often met surreptitiously at night (while under police surveillance) in gas station parking lots to exchange packages. Ford may take in his own dry cleaning. But clearly, there were other errands that he preferred to outsource.

And here's the weirder thing: Given all we now know about the Rob Ford saga, it seems that the mayor might have been on far safer ground if he'd simply cut out the middle man and gone and done his unsavory errands himself. We don't know what was in that pipe he was caught on video smoking—but it now seems clear that it really doesn't matter: The police evidently have no interest in prosecuting the mayor for drug crimes, and the question of whether or not the mayor is a drug user actually doesn't seem to be a top-of-mind question for

Toronto voters. If, on May 17, after Gawker.com first reported being offered the "crack video," Rob Ford had simply stood in front of a microphone, declared that he "has some serious lifestyle issues" he "needs to work out," shrugged, and left the stage, he likely would have survived the scandal—even if the video he then said didn't exist had been posted to YouTube that very day.

But that wasn't the course Ford chose. His fateful choice—and especially Ford's apparent decision to enlist Lisi, a man already known to police, as his fixer—is what let spew an avalanche of dirty laundry, including the court-ordered barrage of the stuff that hit media websites on Thursday morning.

In this age, traditional lifestyle sins of the Fordian variety—gluttony, alcoholism, rage-aholism, even illegal drug use—often get passed over with a yawn or stuck on You-Tube for a laugh; especially in the case of an anti-elitist such as Toronto's mayor, whose imperfections are worn as a badge of authenticity. In many cases (and this seems like it may become one of them) it is the procedural crimes, such as obstruction of justice, that are taken most seriously by the police—because those are the indiscretions that impede investigations into the truly serious trophy criminals targeted by the constabulary.

The only reason Lisi came under police surveillance this year, remember, is because of a much larger, high-priority police initiative—Project Traveller—that targeted drug-and gun-running criminal gangs, including members of the Dixon City Blood cell, whose extensive contacts with Lisi take centre stage in the police document released this week. And it is through this investigative avenue that authorities decided to lay charges against Lisi for extortion, in connection with his alleged attempt to recover the recording.

Now that the wheels of justice have turned this far, Ford may be vulnerable from all sorts of angles. Who knows, for instance, what Lisi may be willing to talk about in return for a plea bargain? And if anything Lisi or Ford has done served to obstruct Project Traveller in any way, even unwittingly, they become vulnerable to the various procedural charges that now seem to attend every modern thumb screwing prosecutorial operation.

How much easier it would have been for Ford if he'd simply told voters "I inhaled," then taken off for a week or two to a rehab centre in Muskoka. Ford would have spent Halloween handing out candy. No one would know the name Alexander "Sandro" Lisi. And the mayor's dirty laundry would not have been waving about on Thursday morning, like some odd sordid flag, in an Etobicoke driveway.

Sad, but hardly shocking

Fri Nov 1 2013
By: Christie Blatchford

The lid has been lifted off something all right. The question is, what is it exactly?

I refer of course to the double whammy of the massive ITO—the Information to Obtain a search warrant—on Toronto Mayor Rob Ford's disreputable friend, Alexander Lisi, which was released by the courts Thursday and the confirmation shortly afterwards from no less a figure than Toronto Police Chief Bill Blair that the notorious video starring the mayor is real and has been recovered.

Though it must have been a satisfying moment for *Toronto Star* reporters Kevin Donovan and Robyn Doolittle, who broke the story of the video in May, shortly after John Cook of the gossip website Gawker published his story, it was hardly a shocker.

Only the most blindly partisan members of Ford Nation could ever have doubted the video existed, or that the three journalists who staked their reputations on the story hadn't seen just what they said they saw.

The video—of a fellow who looks for all the world like Mayor Ford smoking what was alleged to be crack cocaine and heard to be making various slurs—was always real. The only issue was would the police find it in the array of cellphones and electronic devices seized in the original Project Traveller drugs and guns arrests in June—and now they have.

It was in Project Traveller that Mr. Lisi's name (and Mr. Ford's too, for that matter) first came up and sparked the offshoot investigation, Project Brazen 2, which targeted them both.

As for the ITO—474 pages were released, but many are blacked out pending further arguments in court—I had the luxury of being able to read it all on a plane.

What it captures better than anything else are the low, diminished lives of the alleged drug user and his alleged connections. The documents don't detail glamorous high flyers. These are sad, small people, Mr. Ford included.

Their lives are about surreptitious meetings in parking lots of schools (one deliciously called the Scarlett Heights Entrepreneurial Academy), at gas stations and along the dark paths of public parks; hurried snacks from fast-food joints and dubious restaurants; hand-to-hand passes of mysterious packages from driver to driver.

In the awkward words of the police, all of this is "indicative to drug trafficking," and that of course is one of the charges Lisi is facing—possession and trafficking of marijuana, as well as one count of extortion in connection with the alleged attempt to retrieve the video.

Project Brazen 2 ran roughly from mid-June until late September, and all that time, the Toronto mayor spent an inordinate amount of time in short, rushed phone calls to Lisi, and taking short, rushed calls from Lisi, and meeting Lisi. Even if they were only talking, say, football, how on Earth did Mr. Ford ever find time to do any actual work? That's the thing about addiction, whether to drugs or football or cigarettes or booze: It's so all-consuming, the beast that won't sleep. The resources devoted to the investigation were extraordinary.

One of the best cops on the job, homicide Detective-Sergeant Gary Giroux, ran a squad of top guns. There were "spin teams" chasing Lisi, who was surveillance conscious and could turn a five-minute drive into a 45-minute one and switched vehicles the way regular folks change pants.

There was a pole camera set up, wiretaps, surveillance by aircraft (until Mr. Ford's Etobicoke neighbours, upon whom there are no flies, began bitching about the noise), even a tracking device sneaked onto Lisi's most frequently used car. I wonder what it all cost; given the manpower, a great deal I'd bet.

At the end of the day, after all that, what the project

snared were two alleged marijuana dealers (Lisi and a dry cleaner from the rinky-dink plaza), a mayor who, instead of friends, appears to know and consort with virtually every two-bit clown with a criminal record in town but who isn't charged with a single criminal offence and appears unlikely to be charged, either.

But is the biggest city in Canada traumatized by all this, as some have said? Only if Canadians are the most delicate creatures in the world. I can certainly see being saddened by the story; it really is a heartbreaker, on several levels. I can even see being amused by it, particularly if you read the ITO, which many times refers to Lisi successfully taking evasive action as him being "misplaced."

Should Mr. Ford resign, as all the major newspapers were demanding Thursday? Probably, he should. Does he surround himself, apparently, with stooges and thugs? So it seems. But for all the diversion of the video, what the ITO describes are a bunch of small-time guys with a weed problem.

The streak of hypocrisy that runs through our country is wide and deep.

When Liberal leader Justin Trudeau this summer admitted he'd smoked weed a few times in the past—setting the precedent for other politicians, including Mr. Ford, to admit that they'd smoked it too—and announced he supported not just the decriminalization but the legalization of possessing small amounts of marijuana, it was to considerable approbation, and even where there was upset, it was mild.

There are many good burghers—in Rosedale, and Forest Hill, and downtown, where I live, and where I can't go out on my leafy street most nights without being transported back to the 1960s by the smell of the stuff— who are more sophisticated and ever-so much smarter than Rob Ford who would have raised a joint, if one can do that, Thursday night, and toasted the demise of Toronto's rotund, pink, embarrassing mayor. And that is not as sordid, but just as unappetizing, as everything else about the piece.

Usual rules don't apply to mayor

SAT NOV 2 2013
By: Christie Blatchford

The bizarre and complicated character who is the Toronto mayor is unlikely to ever face criminal charges in connection with the notorious crack video.

Rob Ford is at this writing still clinging stubbornly to office, the ship who simply won't sink, though that could change at any moment, given the mercurial nature of both story and man.

But though Toronto Police have the video, seized during raids last summer and successfully recovered only this week from a file someone had tried to delete, the only criminal case in which it may ever star as evidence involves Alexander "Sandro" Lisi, the mayor's friend and sometime chauffeur.

It was the 35-year-old Mr. Lisi who first popped up on the wiretaps which ran during Project Traveller, a major Toronto guns-and-gangs investigation which wrapped this June with raids at dawn and mass arrests.

Mr. Lisi now faces marijuana trafficking charges and another of extortion in connection with an alleged attempt to retrieve a video, which is widely presumed to be the one showing the mayor smoking a substance alleged to be crack cocaine.

Mr. Lisi was released on $5,000 bail on the latter charge Friday.

Mr. Ford isn't captured on those wires.

The 474-page Information to Obtain a search warrant, commonly called an ITO, which was released earlier this week by court order is heavily censored.

But despite the tantalizing prospect of more to come—media lawyers are fighting to get the blacked-out information released—sources say the most damaging details from the ITO about Mr. Ford are already in the public domain.

This massive document contains sufficient lurid detail to ruin an ordinary man, even an extraordinary one, not to mention the most recognizable politician in the city and probably, because of his own past scrapes with the law and notoriety, the most vulnerable one.

Mr. Ford was seen hanging with the disreputable Mr. Lisi and many dubious others with criminal records. He was photographed and tailed by police as the two met at gas bars and the like to exchange suspicious packages or disappear into parks apparently, as a friend of mine puts it, to "drink Purple Jesus like a couple of 15-year-olds," and was even caught in one act of public urination.

If in the ITO police readily identified Mr. Lisi's behaviour as typical of drug dealers and some of the transactions between the two men as suspicious, they weren't apparently so obvious as to warrant arrest on the spot.

Determining that magic moment—the point in any investigation when cops figure they've got all they're going to get and have reasonable grounds to make an arrest—is tricky, less science than art.

And in fact, when a couple of times officers moved in afterwards to search the areas where the two men had met, what police found wasn't evidence of drug use, but empty bottles of vodka.

The usual unwritten rules of the political game— being caught in mortifying if not illegal conduct and resigning in shame—have never appeared to apply to Mr. Ford in any case.

He has already said he sees no reason to quit and may well attempt, says a source who knows him well and has a grudging affection for him despite his abundant flaws, to simply put his head down and bull on through yet another crisis.

Mr. Ford, says this source, is full of contradictions—a so-called man of the people, who has made a name by returning constituents' phone calls into the wee hours, who has virtually non-existent people skills himself.

He is shy, but also a traditional type-A personality with an explosive temper and, the source says, a streak of narcissism, at his most aggressive when he's cornered or confronted by irrefutable proof of his own gaffes, mistakes or bad behaviour.

To borrow a line from the late hockey player Carl Brewer, who said something like this about the disgraced hockey czar Alan Eagleson, Mr. Ford appears to have few friends, only stooges, cronies and goons.

"Broken people," the source says, many of whom hung out with Mr. Ford because he's the guy picking up the tab at the bar, or because they're hoping to sell something to him.

In that crowd, the source says, Mr. Lisi stuck out: He appeared to be "watching the spectacle" of the very bunny he's alleged to have wound up, rather, I suppose, like the whole city is doing now.

Pitiable Ford drags us all down; Press has hardly covered itself with glory

Tue Nov 5 2013
By: Christie Blatchford

"Mayor Ford, have you smoked crack cocaine since you were elected?" This was the question shouted at Toronto Mayor Rob Ford Monday during press scrum outside his office.

I know it's a circus—and yet important.

I know that in large measure Rob Ford brought it on himself and that his apologia via the airwaves Sunday was weird and dreadful because I listened to every word on the way home from a half-marathon in Hamilton, an exercise infinitely less painful if of approximately the same duration.

I know my colleagues, especially those who work at City Hall, are frustrated with this target who never stays still long enough to answer a real question and whose idea of a press conference substitute is to cold-call favoured radio talk shows or writers.

I know there are a thousand questions he hasn't begun to answer, and that he failed to answer them most recently Monday morning (for Mr. Ford, by Tuesday this undoubtedly will qualify as being "in the past") as he made the rounds of a few radio shows.

Sample from the John Oakley show, as follows. Question: "Have you used crack?" Answer: "Johnny, I'm not a drug addict."

So what was he doing hanging around a crack house, then? What does he know or remember about that now-infamous picture of him with three young men, one of whom ended up dead? Why was Mr. Ford spending so much time with Sandro Lisi, the man now charged with extortion in connection with attempting to retrieve the notorious crack video, in parks and gas stations and parking lots? Why did Mr. Ford apologize only for those specific incidents of appalling conduct where he was caught dead to rights and which already had been made fully public, either through reportage or the release of court documents or email last week? Does he have any independent recollection of these events, or were the accounts of same news to him also? As the unidentified colleague I quote off the top put it, has he smoked crack since taking office? Etc., etc.

I know all this and yet I have to say, the more the

pile-on continues, the worse I feel for the poor SOB, and the more I want a shower.

The more we, and by this I mean the collective we—Mayor Ford's colleagues, the callers to all those phone-in shows and the press—engage in this sordid discussion, the lower our own standards inevitably get.

The mob scenes of cameras outside his office; worse, the mob scenes outside his home; and the giggles, smirks and shrieked inquisitions from reporters hardly cover the profession with glory. The smarmy, breathtakingly unctuous remarks from some of his City Hall opponents (urging him to quit or step aside "for his health," or "for the sake of his family"), particularly those who have an interest in the next mayoralty race, are transparent horse manure. If those people are really concerned for Rob Ford the human being, let them speak to him in private.

It seems to me that there are a couple of story lines here.

The biggest, of course, is the mayor's own conduct, his failure to answer for it, and the impact, if any, that has on city business. But existing simultaneously is the fact that Mr. Ford has indeed been subject to unprecedented scrutiny.

This is again partly because he is who he is, partly because the media have changed so dramatically in the past few years, but also because he really was always seen by the city's governing class as a boob who didn't belong.

Once he did the unthinkable and won the election, there really was a loose consensus of the city's best progressive minds, as I feel sure they would call themselves, determined to make his first term his last and to give him the roughest ride imaginable.

That the mayor himself aided and abetted their cause doesn't mean there wasn't a group of movers and shakers who was embarrassed by his election and on the hunt for dirt. (Note: This is not akin to a plot or conspiracy against him. Such a thing isn't necessary with the forces of conventional Canadian thinking, whose numbers are legion and healthily represented in the press.) I know the mayor is not a victim, but I'm damned if I don't sometimes see him that way.

I view his apparent substance abuse issue, whatever the substance or substances, through the lens of my own not insubstantial experience.

Like most people with a wide streak of addiction running through the familial DNA, with a mother who was an alcoholic, I know a couple of things.

The first is that you can take an addict to the front steps of the rehab place, but you can't make him or her walk through the door.

That ain't going to happen unless and until the mayor determines he needs help (and that's assuming he does have an addiction problem, as opposed to a purely behavioural one). All the murmurs of concern and protestations of love and support don't mean squat to someone still in the throes of overpowering need.

The second is that it's a lucky minority who can do it themselves and quit the thing, whatever it is.

And the third is, addicts lie—all the time, about everything, about the stuff that doesn't matter a bit and the stuff that really counts, and particularly about how much or how often they drink or use, and about their alleged intentions to stop.

In vino veritas, my arse.

Is the Ford boil lanced?

WED NOV 6 2013
By: Christie Blatchford

The clown prince of Toronto City Hall is not dead yet.

All those who have been preparing Toronto Mayor Rob Ford's political coffin lo these many months are left, rather like the long-suffering hockey fans of this city, with nothing but the bitter ash of premature celebration in their mouths.

It was as though the boys on the fictional island in Lord of the Flies missed when they threw the great rock at Piggy, and that as they were about to bring the pale, plump fellow down, he ducked and lived another day to bear their taunts.

Just when it appeared Mr. Ford was finally fully cornered, mostly by his own belated admissions—that why yes, now that you ask in the right manner, he has as it happens smoked crack cocaine, probably "in one of my drunken stupors," and that further, he's as curious about that darned crack video as everyone else because he wants to see just how addled was his state because he was so wasted he has no actual memory—the mayor instead late Tuesday announced he was staying on.

With the earlier-in-the-day blockbuster confession that he'd smoked crack, Mr. Ford then told a room stuffed with reporters, "I know I embarrassed everyone in this city, and I will be forever sorry."

If the crack confession appeared unscripted and to take everyone by surprise, including Mr. Ford's own lawyer and staff (some of whom were earlier in the day optimistically talking about "lowering the temperature" at City Hall), the deliberate announcement that followed was probably more of a shocker because in the four hours between the two events, most observers and pundits were confidently predicting the mayor would at least step aside to seek help, if not outright resign.

Only Dennis Morris, lawyer for Mr. Ford and his family, guessed right, telling CP24 moments before his client spoke the second time, "All I know, and you should know by virtue of his past, I'd be surprised if he wants to leave his job."

As the mayor began speaking to the whirr of all those cameras—it sounded for all the world like the dark noise the late William Golding described as "the steady shrill cheering of the tribe"—he described his earlier-in-the-day confession as "the right thing to do" and said he felt "like 1,000 pounds have been lifted off my shoulders."

"I cannot explain how difficult this was to do," Mr. Ford said, adding, with that weird verbal tic he has of slowly repeating words to underline his sincerity, "I hope, I hope, that nobody, that nobody, has to go through what I have gone through."

"I know what I did was wrong, and admitting it was the most difficult and embarrassing thing I have ever had to do."

"Folks," he promised, "I have nothing left to hide."

For a guy with little recollection of his own behaviour and with media lawyers in court that day winning the right to seek the release to the public of the blacked-out parts of the massive search warrant that last week detailed the five-month-long Toronto Police surveillance of Mr. Ford's friend and sometimes driver, Sandro Lisi, and the mayor himself, that was a profoundly risky pledge.

Mr. Ford closed his remarks by saying, "I love my job. I love my job, and I love this city, and I love saving taxpayers money and I love being your mayor."

He said he wants Torontonians to decide, in the October 2014 election, "whether they want Rob Ford to be their mayor."

"Again," he said, "I sincerely, sincerely, sincerely apologize."

His final line, before leaving the podium, was, "God bless the people of Toronto," the same sign-off he and his brother, City Councillor Doug Ford, use often on their weekly radio show.

The line provoked derisive laughter from the enormous crowd of media, and if that is unsurprising in a determinedly secular society like Canada—unlike in America, where politicians routinely invoke such blessings—it may have also hinted at the nature of the gap between Ford Nation and the mayor's natural enemies. It's wrong for him to embarrass the office and the city; it's fine for the press to sneer at him when he invokes a corn-pone blessing.

(Doug Ford himself set the first fireworks off Tuesday, criticizing Police Chief Bill Blair for confirming the existence of the crack video. Councillor Ford is saying he will ask for the chief's behaviour to be investigated, has suggested he should step aside and hints at a conspiracy. I doubt that, but suspect the police chief, as have so many, simply decided on some internal level that it was time to add a push toward the mayor doing what the collective wisdom says is the right thing.)

It was to Mr. Ford's back that the shouted questions that will plague him and this city for the foreseeable future began with a howl: "Why won't you resign?" and "Will you address the racism and homophobia in the video?", the latter a reference to remarks Mr. Ford reportedly made while smoking crack.

Did the mayor, in the words of his lawyer, begin to "lance the boil" with his confession, and set in motion his curious version of rehabilitation? Perhaps, but bets are the boys on the island are even now looking for other rocks to throw at the guy that one of his constituents, interviewed on the tube Tuesday, kindly described as "delightfully human." The delight may be wearing awfully thin, but oh my, the humanity is undeniable.

As the Alcoholics Anonymous prayer—and wouldn't that be a test of the group's code of confidentiality if Mr. Ford were to show up for a meeting—puts it, "God grant us the serenity to accept the things we cannot change, courage to change the things we can, and wisdom to know the difference."

Ford saga doesn't shame Toronto; Self-important rhetoric inflates city's status

THU NOV 7 2013
By: Christie Blatchford

For days now, all that has been running through my poor tiny head is a line from an old Sylvester the Cat and Tweety Bird cartoon, where Sylvester has tried and failed to kick the butt of a creature he believes is a giant mouse (it is a kangaroo) and Sylvester Jr., his kid, moans and says, at least as I hear it in my head with his dad's endearing lisp, "Oh father! I'm so ashamed!" Clearly, I am a person of low intellect and humour both.

But I have to say, the notion that Toronto has suffered a huge blow to its honour or reputation or standing—well, to something anyway—because of Mayor Rob Ford's admission he's smoked crack cocaine is killing me.

I recognize that I'm supposed to be ashamed, because all around me people are saying so, whether it's the Save Toronto group chanting, "Hey hey, ho ho, Mayor Ford has got to go!" outside City Hall, or Toronto Councillor Janet Davis talking about the "damage to this city and this institution," or a TV type demanding the serious makeup before going on.

As reader Chris Rutledge put it delightfully in a recent note, "Lisa LaFlamme, the CTV head newscaster, on the main evening broadcast, opened with a script delivered with Mansbridgian gravitas, to the effect that this was a sombre day for democratic institutions in Canada as Toronto city council and the Canadian Senate dealt with the disturbing spectacle" of blah, blah, blah.

"To which," Mr. Rutledge said, "one might respond, 'Show us two political bodies with a greater public perception of expensive, non-productive irrelevance.'

"Not that this stopped the intonations of, 'A great city like Toronto is now adrift—and the subject of ridicule the world over.'"

The late-night comics are having at us! They're laughing at us on the BBC! Parents are having to tell six-year-olds about crack! I don't care. I can't make myself feel ashamed or embarrassed.

For one thing, it's not me who has smoked crack.

For another, this is Toronto we're talking about, for God's sakes. Don't you have to have an actual reputation before you can be slandered?

I have lived in this city since 1967, when it was a right proper provincial burg, with Sunday no-drinking laws and horrible restaurants where gentlemen who arrived without ties were sometimes handed cheap stained ones before being allowed into the dining room.

As a teenager, I'd sometimes accompany my Dad to the liquor store, all of which were suitably grim little holes where you had to fill out a form, write down the booze you wanted by brand, sign the form and then hand it gravely to the guy behind the counter, who would wrap it in the paper bag that marked you as a loser.

My father would always sign with a fake name—his protest against such stupidity—usually as one or another of the former Canadian prime ministers, dead or alive.

Things are vastly improved now, of course, but that is in no small thanks to the steady influx of people from other parts of the world that are not Toronto who have brought with them the civilizing influences of their native lands and towns.

And, as with so much, it is also a bit of a Pyrrhic victory: Now, you rarely see a man in a suit and tie in a Toronto restaurant, and now, the liquor stores are Gappier than the Gap and advertise their beautifully decorated bright spaces and smart, attractive customers better too. The ads make me feel badly for not drinking enough.

The sole advantage of being old is that I have a memory that goes back more than five minutes, which is a long time by current standards.

Mr. Ford is hardly the first mayor to call international attention to the city, though I confess that most in my lifetime were so dull or inarticulate they could barely command attention in the city.

And neither is his brother Doug, a councillor, the first to take a shot at a police chief.

Why is everyone carrying on as though all this was happening for the first time in history?

Doug Ford is being roundly taken to task for daring to suggest that when Toronto Police Chief Bill Blair last week confirmed the existence of the notorious crack video starring the mayor and pronounced it disappointing, he may have been being a tad political.

Are you kidding me? The job of big-city police chief is inherently political.

For another, police chiefs and mayors, and sometimes even police chiefs and the heads of their civilian police boards, have a long history in this town of battling among themselves.

Most famously, former chief Bill McCormack and the chair of his board, Susan Eng, were all but engaged in open running gun battles in the early 1990s.

As for city council, the proposition that it is an institution worthy of great regard, whose tremendous work is suffering now, is frankly ludicrous.

I have seen city councillors give the boot to civilians who dared enter their special elevator; watched as delegations of citizens are kept waiting so long for their appointed few minutes at the mic that they wither; I have seen council meetings go on for days to no purpose because the elected won't shut up.

I give you the words of my reader-writer, Mr. Rutledge.

"If the mayor were to step aside, is there any substantive case to be made that insightful, focused and productive decision-making would spontaneously arise at Toronto city council? This seems to be the smug assumption among many councillors: We, the decisive and wise crew, able to steer the ship of city greatness—but for the drunken captain!" Whatever happens, whether Mr. Ford stubbornly stays in office, yields to the pleas for his health (some of them issued by those who are after his job or at least have dogs in the next mayoralty race), is outmanoeuvred by council and left in splendid isolation, or is dragged down by the hounds of the press (some of whom would, as another reader said this week, cheerfully water board him if they could), brings no disgrace to the city he leads.

A friend's tears, a mother's defence, another apology; Paying for latest Ford video puts media on perilous path

FRI NOV 8 2013
By: Christie Blatchford

When I watched the brand new, *Toronto Star*-bought and-paid-for video of Mayor Rob Ford in full, mad, out-of-his-mind flight, and the poor sap's brave but foolish scrum with the press now permanently camped outside his City Hall office shortly afterwards, I phoned a friend who spent some time in the U.K. as that country's newspaper phone hacking scandal was developing.

The tradition in Canada is that newspapers don't buy news or pay sources, let alone hire folks to intercept cell phones and email accounts and the like.

Though the whole Mayor Ford story has seen the

266

journalism landscape in this country shift, this is still a significant moment: the first time, to my knowledge anyway, that a major Canadian newspaper has paid for news, or at least frankly acknowledged doing so.

I wanted to formally mark, with someone who understood, what I called the beginning of the end. My friend corrected me, and suggested the beginning is well in the rearview mirror by now.

The video in question shows a staggeringly under the influence of something Mayor Ford on a profane and incoherent rant in an unidentified living room on an unidentified date.

(It is a dreadful, embarrassing bit of tape, though I confess, as my boss and I discussed it Thursday, I swore as much and undoubtedly sounded as engorged with rage as did Mr. Ford. "Don't forget to mention you're sober," said the boss.)

In any case, the poor schmuck was too dumb or too done in to notice that one of those in the room with him was filming him.

The same seems to have been true of the notorious video of Mr. Ford allegedly smoking crack, which according to the *Star*'s chief investigative reporter Kevin Donovan the paper had at one time "certainly" considered buying.

But back then, the paper didn't, and the video disappeared for months until its existence was confirmed last week by Toronto Police Chief Bill Blair. The crack video remains out of the public domain.

This new number apparently was also being shopped around, with the *Toronto Sun* sent two short excerpts as a taste of the product.

Thursday, less than a half-hour after the *Sun* posted an online story about the video, the *Star* posted the whole schmear on its site.

In the accompanying story was a single line that read, "The *Star* purchased this video."

I sent a quick email to Michael Cooke, the paper's immensely likeable editor, partly because I knew the reporters working on the story would be up to their eyeballs, but mostly because significant decisions are the purview of the top dog.

I asked how much the *Star* had paid.

Cookie, as he is called by all and sundry, saucily replied that the "first time you read the amount will be in the *Star*."

Later in the day, I saw CP24's Stephen LeDrew ask him the same question.

"We paid for the video as we pay for lots of things, as you do," Cookie said. "Absolutely," said Mr. LeDrew. (I have no idea what he meant. As someone with the proverbial face for radio, I've no clue what broadcast practices are.) "No one's getting rich off the payment," Cookie added.

Mr. LeDrew tried again, and Cookie again replied that "no one's getting rich. . . . We paid what we normally pay for a video of that nature [where there is] overwhelming public interest."

Well, to borrow from an old line about a whore: We've established what you are, darling, we're just haggling about the price.

(That turned out to be, according to a later story on the *Star* site, $5,000. Cookie described it as akin to the paper buying a book excerpt.)

And what would be the nature of that overwhelming public interest?

Didn't the world know already that the Toronto mayor has, at the least, a whopping drinking problem and is prone to what even he this week called "drunken stupors"? Haven't we known for months (and the sensible among us accepted as fact) that he has smoked crack at least once and aren't many of us skeptical about the once?

The *Star* has led the way on this story—it was the first in the mainstream press to suggest Mr. Ford had substance abuse issues, to disclose the crack video and to document instances where he has appeared out of control. Cookie has injected real oomph into the paper's newsroom and he and the staff deserve much credit.

But paying for a video that merely confirms the worst about a man in free fall puts us onto another path.

At London's Central Criminal Court, eight people are now on trial, five of them top journalists at the now defunct *News of the World*. Charges include conspiring to hack the cell phones of celebrities and private citizens (including the voice mails of murdered teenager Milly Dowler) and bribery.

Interestingly, the report of the inquiry headed by Lord Justice Brian Leveson—its first phase ended last year, the second on hold pending the criminal trials—documented the widespread practice of newspapers paying "third parties" or "contributors" for editorial content or pictures.

Buying news videos doesn't lead to phone hacking, of course. I'm not saying that and neither did the inquiry. But it's a big step in this country, and attempting to characterize it as otherwise is disingenuous.

Mind you, as the fellow I called to mark the moment said, the race to the bottom is well underway.

The petulantly shouted question to Mayor Ford Thursday ("Why won't you just go away?") and the slavering mob of reporters turning up at his house and on duty outside the glass doors to his office—little of that is in the public interest.

Two men have managed to hit notes of decency in the whole shabby piece.

One is the federal Finance Minister, Jim Flaherty, an old Ford family friend, who teared up when he was asked for his "reaction" to Mr. Ford's troubles. The other is Deputy Mayor Norm Kelly, who has tried to strike a kind balance and cautioned reporters that the new video is without context and called it "a private moment."

He is absolutely right: This, now, in our world, is what it means to have a private moment.

When I said I was honest, I was lying; All my actions are due to one person: my assistant

Sat Nov 9 2013

By: Andrew Coyne

(NB: This is not about any particular person in the news. It is about everybody in the news.)

This is the hardest thing I have ever done. This has been the worst experience of my entire life. Believe me, no one feels more badly about this than I do. How could this have happened to me?

I just want all the facts to come out. I'm just trying to get to the bottom of all this. I am prepared to answer everyone's questions. I am prepared to speak with certain hand-picked media. But first let's let the police do their work. Let's see all the evidence. Let's release all the documents. And then let's let my lawyers move for a mistrial.

About my expense claims. We're still trying to piece together what happened, but it seems that, yes, in the crush of a very busy schedule, some receipts marked "personal" or "private" may have been inadvertently mixed in with some other receipts marked "business" or "naughty." And I pledge to you today that every penny of these expenses will be repaid, with interest, out of the proceeds of future expense claims.

Second, with regard to my alleged drug use. I can't lie to you: When I told you I couldn't lie to you before, I wasn't telling the whole truth. But that's because you didn't ask the right questions. When I said "I do not do drugs," you didn't specifically ask, "Are you lying to us?" But let's not overstate this. I am not "addicted" to drugs. If I did drugs, it was only while filling out my expenses.

As for the rest—the conflict of interest, the drunk and disorderly, the theft under, the driving while, not to mention tariff items 13485 through 13496: I am sorry. I am so sorry. I am just so sorry. I am sorry in a hundred inadmissible ways. To my family, my constituents, and most of all, to my dealers, I want to say: I am sorry. I know I've let you down. Worse, I've let myself down. I have not lived up to the standards I set for myself, which were pretty much non-existent to begin with.

I just wish I could go back in time and make every-thing right. If I could go back in time—if I could get in a time machine right now and go back to certain points in my life and change the course of history, without accidentally murdering my own grandfather or otherwise tearing a hole in the fabric of space-time, I would. But I can't. I can't alter the past. On the other hand, I can refuse to learn from it.

All I can do now is apologize and move on. The way I see it, that's the only option open to me, other than, say, accepting the consequences of my actions. Sure, I could plead that I came from a broken home, that I suffer from a rare neurological disorder, that I'm the victim of racial prejudice, that I was set up. But I'm not here to make excuses. My actions are the fault of one person, and one person only: my executive assistant. But she suffers from severe mood swings, so I really don't think you can blame her.

I don't want to seek refuge within the letter of the law. I'm not going to argue, though I could, that the rules did not specifically prohibit claiming millions of dollars in unreceipted "supplies." I'll simply say that if we are going to cast out of public life every expense-fiddling, drunk-driving crack-house found-in who hangs out with gangsters and occasionally utters death threats, it will be impossible to get good people to go into politics.

Were mistakes made? Yes. Mistakes were made: unspecified mistakes, by unnamed people, in the indeterminate past. Am I a perfect person? No. I am not a perfect person. If it's perfection you want, find yourself another guy! But that doesn't mean I can't change. In fact, I have entered treatment for my tendency to blame others, or rather my assistant has. With any luck, I will be back in denial within the month.

And so, I ask only for forgiveness. I place my trust in the people. My fate is in their hands. And when I say the people, I don't mean the fancy people downtown. I don't mean the Ottawa elites. I mean the people who work hard, play by the rules and pay their taxes, and who are therefore accustomed to picking up the tab. Let's not get all high and mighty here.

Let's not get all holier than thou. Let he who is without sin. Judge not, lest ye be judgmental. Who among us has not exchanged suspicious packages with known drug dealers in a 7-Eleven bathroom without acknowledging each other's presence? Which of us would not expense our leg-overs—err, layovers—if we thought we could get away with it? Come on. You know you would. Just admit it already.

It's time to turn the page. It's time to get back to doing the people's business. It's time to let me off the hook. Why should I be allowed to stay on? No. 1, I love this job. I really, really love this job. It completes me. It had me at hello. You think whoever you found to replace me would love this job as much as I do? They could have any job!

God, I love this job, in part because of the opportunities it provides for frequent drug assignations. But that's all in the past. I can assure people, hopefully it doesn't happen again.* I more or less guarantee it.

In short, yes, I do—used to do—a lot of drugs. Yes, I spent a lot of the public's money. Yes, much of it on the drugs. And I expect to be held accountable for it, in the only way that makes any sense: with some sort of plaque. Because you can take away my credit card, but you will never break my records.

*Note: ACTUAL QUOTE.

An early, bitter Christmas for the Ford-haters

SAT NOV 9 2013

By: Rex Murphy

Ever since Rob Ford became Toronto's mayor in 2010, certain people have wondered how he manages to retain his "inexplicable popularity."

The curled lips of Toronto's establishment contrast starkly with the actual poll numbers, which actually went *up* in the days following confirmation that Mr. Ford's infamous "crack video" was the real deal.

It was beyond the conception of the city's elites that someone so visibly gauche, so palpably a "man of the people," with his untidy ways, hulking presence and undisciplined habits, could command such a large swath of public approval and, indeed, public affection.

His aversion to certain exercises of agreed upon political correctness (every mayor *must* attend Gay Pride) appalled the Twitteratti, his almost childlike simplicity of purpose—"end the gravy train, "champion the little guy"—was held up for mockery on Facebook. He was lowclass (despite his family's business success), and so much less educated than that fellow they elected in Calgary.

Rob Ford embraced that other yeti of the Canadian public stage, the id of Canadian hockey itself, Mr. Don Cherry. The *Hockey Night in Canada* icon attended and celebrated Mr. Ford's inauguration (whereas any sensitive modern mayor in the David Miller mould would have reached out to David Suzuki). "Louche"—a word that Mr. Ford himself, needless to say, would never use—doesn't begin to describe it. (It's worth noting, that Don Cherry—still, by the way, without an Order of Canada—irritates the same set even more strongly than Mr. Ford does.)

What the elites have not grasped is that, notwithstanding his various lifestyle sins, Mr. Ford has the gift of projecting a very basic and powerful political message: that he understands, and represents, the majority of people who do not have newspaper columns, or well-read Twitter feeds, or morning shows on CBC.

Ford was an outsider to the elite media game. And being an outsider is something almost every ordinary citizen feels nowadays. Government is not for them. Instead, it's something for containing and managing them, talking down to them, pushing them aside when convenient and then sucking up to them when vote time comes.

Thus, these same voters see in the attacks on Mr. Ford not a little touch of contempt hissed at them for electing him in the first place.

As the stories about Ford piled up, and the campaign to get rid of him grew more zealous and frenzied, this feeling has increased. This was not your ordinary press coverage: This was bear baiting.

And there was money behind it, too: On Friday, the *Toronto Star* admitted that it had paid for the most recent Ford video. Would they have paid up if someone else had come calling with, say, an embarrassing video of Justin Trudeau?

Mr. Ford's supporters, even while admitting the truth of some of the revelations, saw a brutality in the coverage. They recoiled at the bitter meanness of the attacks on the man's weight. And they cringed at the crapulous insults, the piling on past all barriers of taste or mercy.

This coverage has taken its toll. Whether Mr. Ford knows it or not today, it's over.

His fall is sad, because beneath the many failings and the turmoil of this man, there were pulses of genuine feeling for the people. He saw Toronto as he saw that beloved football team he once coached. As he said frequently, he "loves this city." Given how much embarrassment he has caused Toronto, it would be daring even to try to imagine what he must be feeling right now. I expect there is no shortage of pain in his heart.

Yet it may be a pyrrhic victory for his opponents.

The members of what is often contemptuously referred to as Ford Nation, having seen their hero attacked so viciously, will return to viewing government as mostly they have always seen it: something run by insiders, by professional social and business climbers, as fenced in by modern paternalism.

A little flame of belief in politics, lit in a territory where it does not easily shine, is going out. The Ford despisers have their bitter Christmas. The rest of us, on the other hand, would like to see some sense of charity extended to the fallen man himself.

More trouble for Ford on two fronts; Mayor's crowded closet yields yet another batch of skeletons

THU NOV 14 2013
By: Christie Blatchford

In the morning, asked by a colleague on the floor of city council if he had yet admitted to all of his problems, Toronto Mayor Rob Ford shrugged his big shoulders and opened wide his arms, stammered a bit, said he really didn't know and then added winningly, "There might be a coat hanger left in my closet."

By mid-afternoon, it was apparent the man is a whopper of a clothes horse.

With the release of previously redacted pages from the massive search warrant in the Toronto police investigation of him, tumbling out of that crowded mayoral wardrobe came a brace of skeletons.

On these two fronts—at City Hall, where councillors publicly denounced him while asking him to step aside, and from the courts, where a judge ordered more documents unsealed—the embattled mayor emerged looking for all the world like a Kardashian wrapped in an episode of *Intervention* inside a bottle of vodka.

The new revelations detail beliefs from those in his inner circle at City Hall, both past and current staffers, that Mr. Ford is an alcoholic who, when disinhibited and without brakes, also dabbles in harder drugs—you can add allegedly OxyContin and cocaine to the crack cocaine the mayor has acknowledged using at least once—makes weepy late-night calls from his father's grave, flies into rages that border on the physical and may have once invited a prostitute into his office.

As well, Mr. Ford is alleged by his former staff to have behaved inappropriately with a young woman who was once a policy advisor in his office and now works at Toronto Hydro.

Calling the behaviour with the young woman inappropriate is putting it mildly: "He claimed to have slept with her. Mayor Ford said, 'I'm going to eat you out' and 'I banged your pussy,'" according to his former communications assistant Isaac Ransom.

Notes of Mr. Ransom's police interview, like others

with the mayor's former staffers, was included in the unsealed documents.

Mr. Ransom also told detectives that after Mr. Ford lost a key subway vote and took a late-night subway ride, he "tried to hit on a woman that was at the station" and asked her out to dinner.

Others told police how the mayor had smoked marijuana in front of a staffer's then-girlfriend at his Etobicoke home, once drank openly while behind the wheel such that a young aide demanded to be let out and hopped a bus home, and that as recently as this past spring, another employee found a joint in Mr. Ford's desk while looking for a file.

None of these staffers, it is worth noting, appeared to in any way have an axe to grind against the mayor.

After stories about the notorious crack video appeared on the Gawker website and in the *Toronto Star* and the investigation into those allegations began, the staffers were approached by detectives and merely co-operated— exactly as the mayor himself is now refusing to do.

Most of them also managed to speak of Mr. Ford with concern and affection despite his sometimes ghastly behaviour.

For instance, several mentioned how distraught the mayor was when, this past May, he received a letter from his beloved Don Bosco football team, saying he wasn't wanted anymore. "The mayor called [former chief of staff Mark] Towhey later on that day in tears," staffers told police. He was "sobbing and completely distraught."

But Mr. Towhey stood his ground when the mayor then wanted to have a party for the players at his house and tried to enlist some of the young staff to help him. He called Mr. Ford and "told him that he cannot do that."

In fact, Mr. Towhey, who was fired this May after the crack video story broke and he told Mr. Ford he must either take a leave or resign, was clearly the role model for the strange workplace that was the mayor's office: Within the law and the propriety expected by taxpayers, Mr. Towhey nonetheless tried valiantly to protect Mr. Ford from himself.

His conduct, and the efforts it seems to have inspired in other staffers, stands as the lone bright light in this seamy story.

But if Mr. Ford took an unprecedented licking both at city council and in the released documents, he kept on ticking.

At first restrained and polite at the council meeting Wednesday, he soon became bellicose, as did his brother, Councillor Doug Ford.

Bumped to the top of the agenda, at the mayor's own insistence, was a motion from Councillor Denzil Minnan-Wong, which called for Mr. Ford to apologize for misleading Torontonians about the crack video, to co-operate with police, answer councillors' questions and to take a temporary leave to "address his personal issues."

Though the motion ended up passing with a huge majority, it was only a symbolic gesture; council has no authority to force the mayor to step aside.

But any chance the discussion would be high-minded evaporated quickly.

At one point, Mr. Minnan-Wong accused the mayor of physically blocking him as he tried to approach the speaker's chair and demanded an apology.

To cries of "Shame! Shame!" from most of the public gallery but with a few hoots of "Opportunist!" and "Want a tissue?" directed at Mr. Minnan-Wong from a cadre of Ford supporters, the mayor adamantly denied having done anything wrong.

What followed then was a series of mini-explosions.

Someone in the public gallery apparently made a rude gesture to Councillor Pam McConnell, who whirled in her seat and cried, "Stop that! Don't you dare do that to me!" As Mr. Minnan-Wong was asking the mayor questions—getting him to admit he'd bought illegal drugs since being elected—and then wrapped up his speech, Doug Ford began heckling him in loud faux whispers: "What? Are you campaigning now?" and then, "Yep, I'm running for mayor."

The mayor's brother then got to his feet to demand Mr. Minnan-Wong say if he'd smoked marijuana or "drank and ever driven?" and then announced that if councillors were honest, "the whole council would stand up" and admit they'd done it.

That got the mayor to his feet, shouting, "Answer the question! I answered it truthfully!" As the speaker called for a short break, a man from the public gallery left, deliberately giving Doug Ford the finger.

Outside City Hall, an anti-mayor demonstration was getting started. Two people, standing close, held two signs. One read, "Step aside."

The other read, ". . . or fall over."

Get rid of this mayor

Fri Nov 15 2013
By: Editorials

Like other newspapers, we have called on Toronto Mayor Rob Ford to step down. In light of this week's fresh allegations (some of which the mayor has admitted are well-founded), we repeat this call. Rob Ford is unfit to hold any sort of public office, much less the mayoralty of Canada's largest city.

Many of the pundits who have called for Mr. Ford to resign have steeped their pleas in a more-in-pity-than-anger tone. The mayor plainly is plagued by a variety of profound personal problems. He does not seem to enjoy a happy life: One of the claims made in the largely unredacted police document released this week is that he repeatedly called a staff member, crying and unhinged, from his father's gravesite. As with many binge drinkers and illegal drug users, his self-destructive indulgences likely are an effort at emotional self-medication. Clearly, the man should get help.

But this Dr. Phil approach to Rob Ford only takes us so far. Lots of people have expressed concern about his reckless lifestyle—including, reportedly, various City Hall staffers (some of whom reportedly were dismissed for their efforts). By all appearances, the mayor—enabled by equally self-deluded family enablers—simply has dismissed this advice as a disguised form of political criticism. As with all addicts, there comes a point in time when the abused bystander (in this case, the city itself) must move on from helping the addict, to protecting oneself from his toxic presence.

The word "protect" is the correct one, because the most recent revelations about Mr. Ford indicate that his actions have not just put his own health at risk, but that of others as well. This week, for instance, Mr. Ford confessed to drunk driving—a crime that kills over 1,000 Canadians every year. It is not necessary to recite here the many lurid details reported by staffers and former staffers in regard to Mr. Ford's binge-drinking habits. (By at least one report, Mr. Ford doesn't just drink before driving—he actually drinks while driving.) The idea that he would endanger the residents of the city he says he "loves" by hitting a vodka mickey before (or while) taking the wheel shows that he lacks the judgment required of any elected official.

Nor is this the only aspect of the mayor's personal behaviour that directly touches on questions of public safety. Many Torontonians were outraged by the fact that their mayor is an admitted illegal drug user. But what is more outrageous are the after-the-fact actions that emerged from that usage: For months, Mr. Ford's closest operative and confidante was Alexander Lisi, who stands accused of a criminal-extortion plot to retrieve a cellphone video of Mr. Ford smoking from a crack pipe in the company of notorious Toronto gang members. Various characters involved in this drama have been beaten and, in at least one case, killed. Mr. Ford currently does not stand accused of having a legally provable role in these events. But his relationship with Mr. Lisi (they exchanged 349 phone calls in the space of 44 days following media reports of the crack video's existence), a known lowlife and former criminal convict, is thoroughly appalling.

Space does not permit a recitation of all of the other allegations that came to light in the recently released court documents—including accusations of vile racist and homophobic commentary, vulgar abuse toward staff members and profane sexual references. Although many of the claims made about Mr. Ford's behaviour have not been proven, the fact that he lied to his constituents about smoking crack for so long has sullied his reputation in the minds of many Torontonians. His refusal to truly take responsibility for his actions by stepping aside is a slap in the face to the city's voters.

The fact that Mr. Ford is getting his 15 minutes of fame on late-night talk shows and in the international media makes it tempting to dismiss the man as a sort of surreal reality show unto himself. (His use of unprintable sexual slang at City Hall on Thursday, and the bizarre context in which he used his wife as a camera prop during Thursday's daily media circus, certainly added a touch of reality TV trash to the proceedings.) But it's important to remember that this man is not some fictional construct: He is a public servant, disgracing the city he purportedly leads.

The travesty of his mayoralty must end, now, with his resignation. If he refuses, more drastic measures may be warranted.

We are hesitant to call on the provincial government, which itself is facing a criminal investigation, to step in and unseat a democratically elected mayor. The proper remedy would be to introduce recall legislation, so the voters can decide Mr. Ford's fate. Without it, it's hard to see any alternative to the province getting involved, if Mr. Ford refuses to leave on his own.

Wife enters fray at latest apology; Police have plenty to answer for

FRI NOV 15 2013
By: Christie Blatchford

By this point in the shlock opera that is the Rob Ford story, it's a given that the Toronto mayor is, to borrow from Wayne Campbell and Garth Algar on *Wayne's World*, not worthy.

He is not worthy of defending. He is not worthy of the benefit of the doubt. He's not worthy of another chance.

What Mr. Ford is is hard bloody work, and after months of duplicity, he has managed to squander the public trust. And with each new low he attains—the bar is now well below the ground—he exhausts even the residue of goodwill that remained for him even after the last of the trust had gone.

So don't cry for him.

But maybe say a prayer for someone else in the future—the next demon-plagued politician or public figure to come along, or perhaps just the next one who is merely unconventional or unpopular with the city establishment—because there sure are some sobering questions about the Toronto Police investigation that has played such a significant role in Mr. Ford's downfall.

As you know, the mayor is not charged criminally with any offence, though as we all have learned, with this boy, never say never.

Indeed the only people who were charged as a result of the five-month-long, resource-rich police probe that was launched in May, after Gawker.com and the *Toronto Star* published stories about the notorious crack video starring Mr. Ford, are Sandro Lisi and the owner of a dry-cleaning shop.

The mayor's occasional, unofficial driver, believed by Mr. Ford's staff to be his drug connection, Lisi is charged with trafficking in marijuana and with extortion, this in connection with an alleged attempt to retrieve the video.

(I confess to some puzzlement here. If you are attempting to sell to the highest bidder a video showing me smoking crack, and I attempt to convince you otherwise, which of us is guilty of attempted extortion? But I digress.)

The more that is released from the massive Information to Obtain a search warrant, which was partially unsealed, by the courts on Oct. 31, with more details pouring into the public domain this week, the more curious does the investigation begin to look.

First, it appears that the probe began purely and solely as a result of the May 16 stories on Gawker and in the *Star*.

According to the search warrant affidavit, two days later, on May 18, homicide Detective-Sergeant Gary Giroux was assigned "to investigate the matter brought forth by the *Toronto Star* and Gawker.com and their allegations against Mayor Rob Ford. Specifically to investigate the existence of a cellphone containing a video of Ford smoking crack cocaine."

Now, I don't pretend to be terribly familiar with what it takes to kick-start a police probe, and I appreciate that the two published stories were detailed and absolutely correct (as I always believed they were), but I would have thought it took more than media reports of bad or even allegedly criminal conduct.

The investigation itself involved five top detectives, special spin teams to follow Lisi, the mayor and others who popped up on the police radar, the installation of a pole camera outside Lisi's home, aerial surveillance, the retrieval of phone records via court production orders and similarly the retrieval of gas station surveillance camera footage, the installation of a tracker that was for some period surreptitiously attached to Lisi's vehicle and the seizure and meticulous going-over of garbage discarded by the two men.

All of the fruits of this labour (including the discovery of McDonald's bags and empty bottles of booze in the garbage seizure and the July 28 note that the mayor had urinated in public) were described in the ITO for several search warrants that were ultimately executed at Lisi's home, parents' home, garage and the dry-cleaning establishment.

The picture it generally painted was of two men, Lisi and Mr. Ford, behaving exactly as you would suspect people involved in drug transactions might behave—a lot of surreptitious meetings in out of the way places, packages or white bags seemingly left by Lisi in Mr. Ford's conveniently unlocked car, surveillance-awareness and the sort of conduct which is, in police lingo, "indicative" of drug dealing.

And yet, except for one occasion where the undercover officers were so alarmed by Lisi's dangerous driving that they had uniformed officers in a squad car stop him and give him a ticket (the search warrant says this seemed to have the desired effect of slowing him down), the police did nothing.

Indeed, and I can't tell you how much this pains me, but it appears that the lawyer Clay Ruby may have had a point when he said furiously after the first ITO release that the police had given the mayor a deliberate pass.

I am reliably informed that on operations like this, as Mr. Ruby said, police routinely make arrests in what looks like mid-transaction.

In this instance, officers would swoop in, place Mr. Ford and Lisi under arrest and secure their vehicles until a judge authorized a search warrant. If they found nothing, they would apologize (it being the mayor) and move on: They had reasonable grounds.

But if they found something—one party had cash in a pocket, the other had drugs, or both had drugs—things would have been much cleaner, both for the police force and for Mr. Ford.

Had the mayor been facing a criminal charge, he would have had the treasured benefits that flow to those accused but presumed innocent: He would have had his day in court, and the press coverage until that time would have been necessarily somewhat muted so as not to prejudice his fair trial.

And the police force—and here I'm not referring to the detectives in the case but the command that gives them orders—would have been able to say, in effect, "Hey, we did our job" and also awaited disposition in the courts.

Instead, what we had on Oct. 31 was Police Chief Bill Blair confirming the existence of the crack video and saying he was "disappointed" by what he'd seen.

All that can be read like this: The police did by the back door—gave the stamp of approval to the disgracing of Mr. Ford and to the notion that this was correct and in the public interest—what for some reason they were unwilling to do by the front, that is, with an arrest and charge.

Shed no tears for Mr. Ford, but as Martha Stewart might say, it's not a good thing. Spare a thought for the next fellow who is subjected to trial in the court of public opinion, aided and abetted by the police.

An object at rest remains at rest

SAT NOV 16 2013
By: Andrew Coyne

No one seems to know how to get Toronto out of its mayoral mess. It is the product of a flawed civic architecture that, in all fairness, never contemplated the existence of a mayor so mountainously incontinent, yet so impervious to shame, as to make his continuation in the office at once both intolerable and inescapable. He must go and yet will not, and he will not go for the same reason that he must.

Not only have we never witnessed brazenness on this scale, we've never even imagined it. Any other public figure would have resigned long ago in the face of even one of the series of increasingly mortifying scandals in which Rob Ford has been the featured player. But then, anyone with the self-respect or the self-awareness to resign would never have amassed such a record in the first place.

He will not resign. And because he won't, Toronto appears to be stuck with him. The council can strip away nearly all of his powers, as it is in the process of doing, but it cannot actually depose him. The province can but will not intervene unless the council invites it to. And the council will not—in part because it suits the political interests of not a few councillors to leave him in place. So: he cannot be abided and he cannot be removed. Not, that is, unless he were to be imprisoned on conviction of a crime (or else missed three consecutive council meetings, one of the few grounds for removal specifically enumerated in the city bylaws). That remains a possibility. The list of crimes to which the mayor has admitted, from driving while drunk to possession of illegal drugs, continues to grow. The list of crimes and misdemeanours of which he is accused by others is even longer. The mayor's vehement denials of these fresh allegations must be weighed against his no less vehement denials of the ones he now admits.

And hovering over all are the mayor's many connections to figures whose taste for criminality is a matter of public record, from the boyhood friends who, like the mayor, never seem to have left boyhood—their only fixed address seemingly their parents' basements, their hobbies a mixture of illicit substances and beating up their parents—to the gang members whose company he has kept on at least one occasion, and with whom he may have smoked the odd bit of crack.

An amazing number of the mayor's acquaintances seem to end up either dead, wounded, on drugs or in jail. And of these, several seem to have taken an interest in the famous cellphone video of the mayor allegedly smoking crack. Of the three alleged gang members in that almost-as-famous photo taken outside the house where the video was shot, one was murdered, some days after his phone—which may have had the video on it—was stolen; a second was shot, but survived; the third is in jail.

The man who tried to shop the video around is also in jail, where he was stabbed by inmates. The house itself was invaded some days after the video's existence was first reported, its inhabitants—again, friends from the mayor's boyhood—attacked by a man armed with an instrument variously reported as a steel pipe or an expandable baton, who accosted them by name and demanded to know where the video was. Meanwhile, the mayor's driver and closest confidant, Sandro Lisi— you will remember him from the police surveillance reports of him and the mayor surreptitiously exchanging suspicious packages in public places—is charged with extortion, apparently in connection with attempts to retrieve the video. At the very least, the revelation that the mayor who advocated a get-tough policy with gangs and a zero-tolerance policy on drugs was himself involved with both gangs and drugs would strike some as hypocritical. But it raises much more troubling questions, not least for the police: When you are in the midst of a year-long investigation of drug gangs, it is unhelpful to discover the mayor is one of the people you have to keep under surveillance. It may be that the police's reluctance to pursue matters further with the mayor is explained by that larger inquiry. Who knows? Maybe the mayor was working undercover.

And yet—there Mr. Ford sits, immovably: disgraced, largely powerless, but still the mayor. Is that his fault? The city's? Or is it the fault of those who put him there in the first place and sustained him through the long train wreck that followed: the staff who failed to report his misdeeds; the commentators who excused them; the partisans who ignored them? Disasters on the Ford scale, we are taught, do not just happen, and while the mayor's endless supply of lies, manipulativeness and sheer chutzpah have helped to preserve him in office until now, he could not have done it alone.

And of all his enablers, the most culpable are the strategists, the ones who fashioned his image as the defender of the little guy, the suburban strivers, against the downtown elites, with their degrees and their symphonies—the ones who turned a bundle of inchoate resentments into Ford Nation. Sound familiar? It is the same condescending populism, the same aggressively dumb, harshly divisive message that has become the playbook for the right generally in this country, in all its contempt for learning, its disdain for facts, its disrespect of convention and debasing of standards. They can try to run away from him now, but they made this monster, and they will own him for years to come.

Get help? He's had plenty.

Fords offer choice of nadir; Mayor menaces the gallery at wild council meeting

TUE NOV 19 2013
By: Christie Blatchford

To the old saw about horseshoes and hand grenades, you may now add Meeting 44, the Nov. 18 special meeting of Toronto city council.

If that wasn't a political castration that a filled-to-the-brim council chamber witnessed, it's close enough to count.

Now, anyone who was there will have her favourite moment, by which I mean complete and utter nadir.

For some it will be when the Brothers Ford—Rob, the now gelded mayor, and Doug, the councillor—turned on Councillor Paul Ainslie, who had invited the attack because he was provocatively, oh, breathing or something at the time.

"Councillor Ainslie," Doug Ford sneered pointedly. "You got your own issues."

At this point, the mayor went into a frantic cartoon pantomime of a man at the wheel, driving off the road.

Grinning like a man unhinged, the mayor hooted at Mr. Ainslie, "Or was it one wheel?" (Earlier this year, Mr. Ainslie received a warning from police after he was pulled over in a RIDE check. He wasn't charged.)

For some, it may be the two occasions when Mayor Ford, sitting in the speaker's chair, tried to get Councillor Ford's attention by saying, "Jones!" and motioning for him to come up to the chair. (The Brothers Ford frequently call each other Jones.)

Others may have embedded in their memories Mayor Ford's closing address, when in his speech against the motion, he invoked the memory of his dead father, self-identified with "the poor people [more] than the rich people," plugged his new show airing that very evening on Sun TV (he promised "my side of things, unfiltered," to which in my head I cried, "But I want you filtered!") and then compared the meeting to the Saddam Hussein–led invasion of Kuwait in 1990.

Imbuing U.S. president George Bush with his own weird tic of repeating that which he means most sincerely, Mayor Ford quoted him telling the Iraqi leader, "'I warn you, I warn you, I warn you' and thundered, "You guys have just attacked Kuwait! This is going to be outright war!"

But for me, the lowest point came much earlier,

when Mayor Ford finished off his questioning of Councillor John Filion, who proposed the motion to strip the mayor's office of cash and power, by noting that Mr. Filion had wracked up more office expenses for his one ward than the mayor had and saying, and this was meant ironically, "Don't you think you have a spending problem?" By this point, many in the packed public gallery were openly chortling derisively or heckling the mayor.

Then, with Doug Ford taking over the questioning, speaker Frances Nunziata trying to direct him and maintain order, Mr. Ford demanded that the "special interests and the CUPEs behind me [in the public gallery] . . . do me a favour" and be quiet.

The mayor from his chair immediately began chanting, "NDP! NDP! NDP! NDP!" and muttering about "socialism."

Very red in the face now, the mayor got up and walked away a bit; he was rocking back and forth on his heels, clearly spoiling for a rumble in the jungle. He approached a strapping fellow who, it was said later, either worked in his office or was a security officer.

"Let's go out in the crowd and talk to them," he told the man. Mayor Ford was again grinning, but also unmistakably bellicose.

The staffer obediently lifted the rope which separates the floor of council from the public section, and out came the mayor, glaring, bouncing on his feet, all but kicking up dust in the bull ring.

At the mayor's explicit instruction, the staffer began filming citizens in the crowd with his cellphone, the mayor occasionally saying, "Did ya get these guys in the back?" and "Get this guy, right here!" All the while, he was smiling ferociously, but there was a profound air of menace emanating from him.

I was in the second row of the public gallery and he walked inches from me, shaking the occasional hand, including that of the man beside me, who said he was an old friend, and giving the odd thumbs-up.

But mostly, with that big, thin, dangerous smile plastered on his face, he prowled the alley in front of the public gallery, daring the hecklers to heckle him in the face, in person.

Finally, a couple of them did.

From the speaker's chair, Ms. Nunziata called a recess, but it was too late to quell either the mayor or the enraged citizens. From the gallery, the crowd began to chant, "Shame! Shame! Shame! Shame!"—and quite correctly too.

Here was the chief magistrate of the city, prowling up and down the public gallery, trying to intimidate the very people for whom he works and who pay his salary, frightening at least one woman, probably in her 50s, into pulling her blue scarf over her face.

"How do you know Anthony Smith, you lying scumbag?" someone shouted, referring to the young man who is a homicide victim and who is one of the three who posed in that now notorious picture with the mayor, outside an alleged crack house. "How do you know Anthony Smith, you lying scumbag?" the man shouted again.

By this point, Doug Ford had joined his brother in the alley, the two of them, bristling with hostility, shouting up at citizens.

"Special interests!" Doug yelled. "Get the real taxpayers down here!" I think it was the woman with the scarf over her face, who sat as if stunned, but someone murmured wonderingly to someone else, or no one, "But I'm a real taxpayer."

To my eyes, it was only the intervention of Councillor Mark Grimes, a big (but gentle) man himself who steered Doug Ford back through the velvet rope, that prevented actual fisticuffs.

Minutes later, back in his seat, the mayor apparently perceived that his brother was under attack and sprinted to his aid, running behind the councillors' row to get there, and in the process, bowling over Councillor Pam McConnell, who went arse over tea kettle.

It was the mayor and his chief of staff who appear to have caught Ms. McConnell just in time, sparing her from cracking her head open.

Afterwards, nursing a swollen cheek and lip, she said with real dignity, "This is the seat of democracy, not a football field."

Amen.

There's only one thing left to say to Ford: Get out; Toronto mayor shows contempt for social norms

Tue Nov 19 2013
By: Andrew Coyne

Something snapped at Toronto City Council Monday afternoon, and it wasn't just Rob Ford's cerebral cortex. Watching the mayor and his brother strutting about the council chamber—ignoring the speaker, taunting other councillors, shouting down city officials, screaming insults at spectators, the whole carried out with an air of anarchic glee—was to sense the last tether connecting our politics to some sort of civilized norms breaking under the strain. We are adrift now, floating wildly, with no idea of where we will end up.

At one point the mayor engaged in an extended pantomime of a drunk driver, directed at a councillor who had been cautioned by police. At another, racing about the chamber—literally sprinting—he ploughed into another councillor, knocking her to the floor, apparently in his haste to join the apprehended brawl then underway between his brother and members of the public gallery.

To add to the general note of menace, the mayor was seen directing his personal driver/security guard, who for some reason was allowed onto the chamber floor, to videotape certain of the spectators who had displeased him. Given the services his last driver, the alleged extortionist Sandro Lisi, is accused of performing, it was an altogether chilling moment.

If it is unclear where we are headed, it is clear as day how we got here. With each passing day, the Fords have been dragging the standards we expect of public officials deeper and deeper into the muck, each past act of public or private depravity somehow normalized by the next, worse offence. It is as if, knowing the evidence cannot exonerate the mayor, they and their apologists have decided to annihilate our very ability to judge the evidence.

Over the past couple of weeks, since it was at last confirmed that, contrary to months of stonewalling and evasions if not outright denials, the mayor was indeed caught on that infamous cellphone video—and his still more belated admission that he has smoked crack—the public's collective moral judgment has been assailed by every sly wheedle, every manipulative tactic, every deliberate lie the two could come up with.

We have seen, by turns, the remorseless apology ("All I can do is apologize and move on"), the bargaining for time ("I have nothing left to hide"), the pseudo-legal clam-up ("I can't say anything, it's before the courts"), the non-denial denial ("I do not smoke crack; I am not an addict"), the Clintonian verb-parsing ("you didn't ask me the right question"), the claim of diminished responsibility ("in one of my drunken stupors"), the appeal to impossible standards ("I'm not a perfect person"), the appeal to no standards ("everybody does it"), the invocation of class envy ("all these rich and elitist people . . . they're the biggest crooks around"), the plea for sympathy ("this is the second-worst day of my life, after the day my father died"), the declaration of pure, all-devouring solipsism ("I love this job"). And that's just a partial list.

The Fords have picked fights, dodged blame, sprayed accusations and issued threats ("If you wanna get nasty we can get nasty," the mayor told an interviewer. "I can start digging up dirt on every single one of those politicians . . ."). The Fords have even demanded that every member of council undergo a drug test, as if that, and not the mayor's documented, multiple misdeeds, were the issue. Throughout, they have tugged on all those sentiments that often cloud the public's ability to form inferences in such cases—judge not, who am I to judge, don't rush to judge, anything but the very thing we are called to do as citizens with regard to those we elect: judge.

Even in the midst of Monday's mayhem, his apologists were holding him to the standard of a Friday night beer league goon: "He was provoked." More culpable still has been the unwillingness of political leaders, notably his federal Conservative allies, to denounce Ford in the terms he deserves. The provincial Tory leader, Tim Hudak, deserves credit for pledging his support for provincial intervention, should that prove necessary. But the Liberal premier has said she will not without an invitation from the council, and the council seems disinclined to issue such an invitation.

The rest of us are, in a sense, handcuffed. We simply don't know how to respond to this level of misconduct, this sort of contempt for social norms. At some level, our whole system depends upon people, however badly they may behave, staying within some sort of limits. But the Fords have demonstrated they are under no such constraint.

All of which should make abundantly clear that it is time to put aside the therapeutic language, the Oprah-like pleas to the mayor to "get help" or "seek treatment."

We are long past that point. The mayor's actions Monday were quite deliberate. They reflected the influence, not of intoxicants, but his own limitless ego and unformed character. As such it is not Ford who has the problem; it's the city. The message he needs to hear, from every corner, is not get help, but get out.

Police could have held Ford: Chief; First lengthy interview on Project Brazen 2

WED NOV 20 2013
By: Christie Blatchford

Toronto police investigating Mayor Rob Ford "absolutely" weren't directed away from arresting him if they saw him do anything illegal, says Police Chief Bill Blair.

"Of course not," Chief Blair told Postmedia News Tuesday in his first lengthy interview about the controversial probe, Project Brazen 2.

"I'd rather not have played any role in this at all," he said Tuesday in his seventh-floor office. "But I'm not sure we were given any choice."

As the Postmedia News has reported previously, it was mention of Mayor Ford's name on wiretaps in another, much bigger investigation—Project Traveller, a guns-and-gangs probe—that sparked police interest.

This was before the Gawker.com gossip website and the *Toronto Star* went public in mid-May with revelations that they had seen a video of Mayor Ford smoking what appeared to be crack cocaine.

Since then, the mayor has admitted to "sometimes" smoking crack while "in one of my drunken stupors," but at the time of the first stories, the allegations were shocking.

It was then that Project Brazen 2, with homicide Detective-Sergeant Gary Giroux at the helm, began, its purpose to investigate the allegations against Mayor Ford and specifically the existence of a crack video.

The four-month investigation culminated in the mayor's friend and sometime driver, Sandro Lisi, being arrested and charged with marijuana trafficking and, later, extortion.

That Mr. Ford himself wasn't also arrested during the course of the probe led some to suspect the mayor had got a free pass.

Yet at the same time, the mayor's brother, City Councillor Doug Ford, lashed out at Chief Blair for publicly confirming that police had recovered the notorious crack video.

Almost unnoticed in this week's installment of the circus at City Hall was the fact that Ontario Superior Court Judge Ian Nordheimer subtly and quietly endorsed the chief's much-criticized handling of the powder-keg video at an Oct. 31 press conference.

The judge described Chief Blair as having "fairly

characterized the contents of that video as being 'consistent' with previous media reports."

Aside from several reporters from the *Toronto Star* and the Gawker.com website, Chief Blair and Judge Nordheimer are among a select few who have actually seen the 90-second video.

The judge's remarks came in a Nov. 18 decision on the Mohammad Khattak case that got lost in massive coverage of the volatile special meeting of city council the same day, where council voted to strip the mayor of power and staff and where the Ford brothers prowled the floor beneath the public gallery, yelling and taunting those they believed were heckling them.

Lawyers for Mr. Khattak, who is one of the Project Traveller accused and also one of three men who posed with Mayor Ford in a picture that has been widely published, had been seeking permission for their client to see the video.

The picture and the video have come to be linked, but a prosecutor confirmed publicly that Mr. Khattak doesn't appear in the video, nor is his voice heard on it.

The judge dismissed the application in his Monday decision.

Chief Blair explained some of the turns the investigation did or didn't take. For instance, he correctly pointed out that though the enormous Information to Obtain a search warrant document, called an ITO, became public, it's "not the police who do that."

When police prepare such a document, used to convince judges that officers have reasonable grounds to search a home or car, it is sealed—only lawyers, in this case many of them acting for media outlets, successfully persuaded Judge Nordheimer to unseal some or all of it.

"We do not release any of the information publicly," Chief Blair said. "We quite correctly put what we knew before the court."

He agreed the document, which runs to almost 500 pages, "is very detailed," but noted that "there was an extensive investigation that took place. All of the information that was gathered . . . went into the ITO.

"I think we had an obligation to full and frank disclosure to the court. But that goes into a sealed document."

It's the court that "will determine what's admissible and what's in the public interest to release.

"That's the way the system works."

Some critics have pointed to the fact that when Lisi and Mayor Ford were under surveillance, and police believed their behaviour was suspicious and "indicative" of drug dealing, they weren't stopped and arrested.

Chief Blair said those decisions are left "to the individual officer" on the ground and in the moment.

But police also noticed that both men were "surveillance conscious"—Lisi and Mr. Ford appeared to suspect they were being tailed. "I think that would have been something the officers . . . had to take into consideration," Chief Blair said. In other words, the two could have been setting a trap for the police.

Much has also been made of the fact that Chief Blair held the press conference in which he confirmed the video's existence on the same day, Oct. 31, that the first block of information from the ITO was released.

But in fact, it was the judge who gave the green light for the document release and prosecutors who had to redact some information in the file—and, as reporters who were waiting for the go-ahead on the edge of their seats know, the documents were first expected to be released on Oct. 30.

Chief Blair learned on Oct. 29 that among the huge number of cellphones, computers, hard drives and laptops that had been seized in the Project Traveller raids was the recovered digital file containing the crack video.

It was turned over to the Project Brazen team of investigators, who consulted, as they had been all along, with senior lawyers at the provincial attorney-general's criminal law office at 720 Bay Street to determine "any charges that would be appropriate."

"When they advised me they were going to lay a charge [the extortion charge against Lisi, allegedly in connection with efforts to retrieve the video], I then sought advice on what information could be, or should be, released," Chief Blair said.

That step isn't as unusual as it may appear, he said: "Actually, it's always prudent. . . . What I was thinking was that I wanted to ensure that we didn't in any way jeopardize the integrity of any prosecution."

The two lawyers he consulted told him it "was appropriate and in the public interest to disclose, but the evidence that was on that video file was not appropriate to disclose . . . it was evidence in a charge we laid that morning."

Asked if investigators considered seeking a warrant to search Mayor Ford's house, Chief Blair said, "I don't know. They didn't indicate they had reasonable grounds to believe it was necessary to do that, but I don't know.

"I never discussed that with them," he said.

"I stay at arm's length from these investigations," he said. "I wasn't receiving detailed particulars of their investigation.

"They go and conduct the investigation and conduct the investigation and pursue evidence as required."

Det.-Sgt. Giroux, he said, "never briefed me."

"I was kept apprised of the progress of their work through Deputy [Mark] Saunders and also Deputy [Mike] Federico."

Chief Blair said the Brazen probe hasn't been "costed" yet, but said that while it was an extensive investigation, many of those working on it were simultaneously "doing other things" and other investigations—the drug squad officers involved, the surveillance teams, and of course the core group of homicide detectives.

"Even Det.-Sgt. Giroux," he said, "was working on that horrific homicide that was solved," the murder of the Eritrean woman, Nighisti Semret, who was knifed to death in October of last year in a Cabbagetown alley on her way home from work.

On Sept. 30 this year, it was Det.-Sgt. Giroux who announced that a man had been charged with first-degree murder in Ms. Semret's slaying, and in the death of another Eritrean woman, Rigat Essag Ghirmay, whose remains were found on May 24 this year.

The intricacies of gang life; Mayor Ford got tangled up in drugs and crack houses

Thu Dec 5 2013
By: Adrian Humphreys

On the night he was killed in a clubland shooting now entwined with the fate of Toronto Mayor Rob Ford, Anthony Smith, known by fellow gang members by his nickname "Grenades," spotted a man with whom he had a beef.

Wednesday night had slipped into Thursday morning amid the thumping hip-hop of the Loki Lounge, a King Street West club promising "Wild Wednesday" parties, when Mr. Smith grew increasingly agitated at the sight of Saaid Mohiadin.

Mr. Smith wanted to hurt him. He tapped out a series of text messages on his phone to Liban Siyad, allegedly a fellow member of the Dixon City Bloods gang, about the plan, police allege in a newly released court document.

A reply came back: "Okay halal meat."

Police believe the message was slang for "dead meat" and signalled permission for Mr. Mohiadin to be killed, they allege.

Minutes later Mr. Smith, with two pals, Mohammed Khattak, known by the nickname "Ali K," and Ahmed Dirie, known as "Santana," confronted Mr. Mohiadin and another man outside the club, police allege.

It did not go well. Mr. Smith was shot in the left side of the head; Mr. Khattak was shot in the chest and neck. As the last man standing, Mr. Dirie quickly contacted Mr. Siyad and told him what had happened, police allege. He claimed the shooter was "Panda," who police believed to be Nisar Hashimi.

The March 28 shooting was an ugly incident, reflecting the violent brinkmanship of a growing guns-and-gang street culture and might have been forgotten in a swelling list of young, black men lost to street violence. Instead, it now marks another landmark on the twisting road of the political and personal scandal of Mr. Ford.

It was suspected drug dealers with the Dixon City Bloods who secretly recorded a video of the mayor on a cellphone camera, apparently smoking crack cocaine and making a homophobic remark, police allege.

Since that push of a cellphone camera button, its very existence hung like a curse over the Dixon neighbourhood.

A murder, other shootings, woundings, kidnapping, threats, blackmail, extortion, break-ins, beatings, police raids, arrests, roving camera crews and nosy news reporters seemed to descend on the neighbourhood at the epicentre of the video scandal, and much of it, rightly or wrongly, was attributed to the sensational Ford video.

Many lives have been shattered. Mr. Smith died during the nightclub shooting.

Mr. Khattak survived but was arrested, alongside Mr. Dirie, in a large police guns-and-drugs probe underway at the time of the shooting. Mr. Hashimi, the friend of the intended victim, was convicted of manslaughter and aggravated assault.

Mr. Siyad, identified as one of the men trying to sell a video, was also charged in the gang sweep. He is also named as the victim of an alleged extortion by Mr. Ford's friend and occasional driver, Alexander Lisi, who police say was aggressively trying to retrieve the digital file.

Mr. Smith and Mr. Khattak appeared with the mayor in a now infamous photograph, used as bait to attract buyers to the Ford video. Police were soon investigating whether there were any links between Mr. Smith's murder and the clamouring to obtain the video.

All of it was going on virtually under the noses of Toronto police, who were in the midst of a large probe focusing on the Dixon City Bloods, codenamed Project Traveller. As soon as Project Traveller ended with the arrest of 44 people, investigators turned their attention to the mayor, an operation codenamed Project Brazen 2.

The overlap between the two probes is striking, highlighting the mayor's purported links to the gang. Of the 59 principal targets of the police's massive drug, gun and gang probe, seven of them became principal subjects in the investigation of the mayor.

Police allegations of those links are detailed in newly revealed portions of an immense summary of a police investigation of Mr. Ford and Lisi contained within a sworn affidavit, called an Information to Obtain, filed by the police in connection with the investigation; the accuracy of the sworn affidavit has not been tested in court.

Captured on the police wiretaps are calls in mid-May from the phone of Mr. Siyad, who police believe was arranging a meeting with John Cook, a news editor at Gawker, a U.S. website, about the mayor's "crack video."

On May 14, there are several calls between Mr. Siyad and a phone belonging to Mohamed Farah, while, police believe, Mr. Cook was negotiating his failed bid to buy the video.

On May 17 at 12:47 a.m., the day after Gawker, followed quickly by the *Toronto Star*, revealed the existence of the Ford video, police intercepted a call from Mr. Siad, identified as one of the men trying to sell the video.

He asked about a phone believed to contain the Ford video that was stored in a red pencil case; he asked a female relative to take it out and hold on to it for him, the document says.

He may have realized the explosive nature of what he had.

Later, on May 29, two men allegedly kidnapped Mr. Siad. The men, allegedly Siyadin Abdi and Ahmed Farah, asked him about the video for about an hour, the document alleges.

Mr. Siad was crying. He said he had destroyed the video and his family was in trouble. He was threatened, told that if he was seen again in the neighbourhood he would be killed, police allege.

When Abdinaim Hussein was told what the pair had done, police allege, he said: "You guys are stupid, you should have really hurt him."

Police did not find independent proof he was kidnapped, but in text messages that day Mr. Siad told friends he had left town, even though he had not, according to police. Messages from his friends became increasingly aggressive.

Even arrest did not protect him. After his June 15 arrest in Project Traveller, Mr. Siad was stabbed in a fight inside the Don Jail with three other inmates. He survived wounds to his back, chest and right cheek.

Others possibly linked to the video also faced violence.

On May 21, Fabio Basso, an old friend of the mayor's and a resident of 15 Windsor Road, where the video is believed to have been recorded, was reportedly beaten by a visitor wielding a pipe who came looking for the video.

That same day, police and paramedics were called to

the 320 Dixon Road apartments. When officers arrived, they found Abdullahi Harun in the front lobby being treated for a gunshot wound.

Mr. Harun had earlier allegedly been heard by police saying he "had Rob Ford smoking on the 'dugga,'" the document says, and had "so much pictures of Rob Ford doing the hezza," usually a slang term for heroin.

In hospital, Mr. Harun told police he was helped down to the lobby by Mr. Siyad. On the 17th floor, officers spoke to a witness who heard shouting in the apartment's hallway. Looking out his peephole, he saw six or seven men arguing. He then heard gunshots and he hid.

Mr. Harun and Mr. Siyad were also arrested in Project Traveller.

After the Traveller arrests, police investigating Mr. Ford and Lisi visited the men believed to also be involved with the video inside jail.

When police interviewed Mr. Farah, he laughed out loud when told they were investigating the mayor. He wouldn't verbally answer any questions, only nod or shake his head in response.

But when he was asked about the mayor's video, he stood up and began knocking on the locked interview door to leave. When asked if he would like to hear one of the wiretaps suggesting he was involved, he stopped knocking and returned to the table, police say.

He was then read police information about the kidnapping of Mr. Siad. He shrugged, shook his head and started knocking on the door to leave. He was let out by a prison guard, the document says.

Mr. Abdi was also uncooperative, police say.

He said he did not remember conversations about a kidnapping and could not explain why his cellphone called the mayor's office on March 18 at 10:16 p.m. When police spoke with Monir Kassim, one of three men with Mr. Ford in the now infamous photo outside the Windsor Road house, he said he had never been there and was not the man in the picture, the document says.

Mr. Siyad told police he was not the man speaking on police wiretaps that were played to him in jail. Mr. Harun would not answer the investigator's questions, the document says.

Mr. Dirie told police that Mr. Smith was his friend. He had seen the picture of his friends with the mayor outside 15 Windsor on Facebook and Instagram before it made its way into the media.

Mr. Dirie agreed his voice is in a wiretapped phone call with the mayor's driver, but he did not know who the driver was, he said. In a conversation, someone said the mayor's driver had told him that Mr. Siyad was "halal meat," the same sentiment immediately preceding the deadly nightclub shooting, the document alleges.

The video also shook the mayor's staff, leading to firings and resignations.

David Price, the mayor's director of logistics and operations at the time, had already received an anonymous phone tip that the Ford video was in the hands of Somali drug dealers who hung around 320 Dixon Road, the document says.

When he heard of the shooting there, he was shocked, he told police, saying he found it "sobering," the document says. In fact, when he heard, it made him think the tip was "probably accurate."

When former aide Mark Towhey heard about the shooting he "became uncomfortable," he told police, describing it as "very problematic for their administration," the document says.

Mr. Towhey then asked Mr. Price how he knew people who would know such things as where the video might be.

"It's a small neighbourhood," Mr. Price replied.

Why the drugs matter

Thu Dec 5 2013
By: Chris Selley

Only the most credulous and inattentive should be shocked by the allegations contained in the unredacted Project Traveller police affidavits released Wednesday.

None of the allegations—from claims that various lowlifes have visual evidence of Mayor Rob Ford in any number of uncomfortable situations to the suggestion Mr. Ford offered $5,000 and a car in exchange for the crack video—have been proven in court. Mr. Ford hasn't been arrested. So . . . status quo, right?

He retains the championship belt of office thus far thanks to the "I'm not perfect, I've made mistakes" gambit. He can't set foot near a sporting venue without being mobbed by adoring . . . fans? Gawkers? Whoever his supporters are at this point, perhaps the camel's back has broken, and no more straws can harm him.

Perhaps. But there's a lesson here, should very stubborn partisans wish to learn it, about politicians and the law.

One of the more ambitious defences employed by Ford Nationalists was this: Drugs are drugs, and we all have vices, and shouldn't Toronto's mayor be entitled to get off his head once in a while?

Even Prime Minister Stephen Harper's spokesman, Jason MacDonald, indulged that equivalency, albeit from a disapproving angle: "Our government does not condone illegal drug use, especially by elected officials while in office, including Justin Trudeau," he said.

In short: Who cares? Why does it matter? Well just look at this unholy criminal mess orbiting around the mayor of Toronto, reaching right into his office. This is why it matters.

"He's keeping company with criminal elements and that could put the whole city in danger, not only himself," Ian Greene, professor emeritus of public policy at York University, told the *National Post* last month, when the first round of redactions was lifted. "Criminal elements could think, 'I've got a friend in public office, maybe I can take advantage of that for my personal gain.'"

He added: "There's a danger that if you're hanging out with people who are involved in criminal activities, then you do risk being drawn into those activities and possibly blackmailed." The allegations unsealed Wednesday suggest all of that happened and more.

You can't buy illegal drugs without consorting with criminals. You can't ingest them without consorting with them indirectly. Whatever steps you might take to ensure you're purchasing ethically sourced or fair-trade weed or crack or heroin, you are associating yourself with a violent underworld in which people fairly routinely get murdered for their troubles. If you're a public official, all of that opens you to every imaginable form of extortion and blackmail.

And if that somehow doesn't bother Ford Nationalists on a moral level, they might consider that it's unlikely to save them any money.

There is no allegation of public funds going directly to deal with this situation (although Mr. Ford's staff do seem to have been paid more and more money as things went more and more off the rails).

But a politician trying to ward off blackmail and personal ruin is unlikely to be giving budget committee meetings his full attention.

Pace Mr. Harper's office, this has nothing to do with Justin Trudeau. But it's worth mentioning that the same principle holds: Illegal activity by prominent individuals invites blackmail. That's why politicians shouldn't do illegal things.

Needless to say, for many reasons—some more logical than others—a video of Justin Trudeau smoking pot wouldn't have been damaging to him, or any other politician.

More to the point, it seems highly unlikely that Mr. Trudeau has surrounded himself with a gang of employees, semi-employees and hangers-on who might undertake a massive illegal effort to retrieve said video from the criminal and gang associates that Mr. Trudeau presumably also doesn't have.

That's why Rob Ford shouldn't be Mayor of Toronto.

Councillors call on police to explain no Ford charges; Mayor says nothing

Thu Dec 5 2013

By: Josh Visser and Natalie Alcoba

City councillors in Toronto are openly calling for police to explain why Mayor Rob Ford has not been charged following the allegations in the latest batch of police documents into the so-called crack video.

Mayor Ford refused to comment to the media as he left City Hall Wednesday, and seemed to laugh when asked if he had used heroin—another claim made in the newly released court documents. He could be seen through the windows of his office that overlooks Nathan Phillips Square earlier, watching a lawyer discuss the breaking news about him on television.

Mayor Ford said, "I have nothing left to hide" after he admitted to smoking crack cocaine in early November.

Councillor Adam Vaughan said this latest wave of allegations—that includes the suggestion that the mayor may have offered $5,000 and a car to two men trying to sell a video that appears to show him smoking crack cocaine—requires Chief Bill Blair to provide an explanation, and soon, about how police managed the investigation, what steps they have taken and why.

"It's wrong to leave an impression in the minds of Torontonians that there are two sets of rules," he told reporters. "Two-tiered policing is not acceptable. A kid like Rob Ford, with a trust fund, gets policed differently? because if that is the case, that's wrong.

"I'm not making an allegation about the police, I don't know the full extent of the evidence . . . [but] there needs to be an explanation," he said.

Councillor Joe Mihevc also urged clarity on the part of police, saying it looks to him like the mayor has "either broken the law or he is on the edge of the law."

"We need to know [from the police] that it is either being fully investigated and that they are in process or that they have concluded their investigation and are about to either lay a charge or to say that no charges should be laid," he said.

Speaking minutes earlier, Chief Blair was mum on whether police were considering charges against Mayor Ford.

"All of the evidence that was gathered in that case has been reviewed by investigators and with Crown prosecutors in this case, and where reasonable probable ground to lay a charge exists, charges have been laid," he told reporters Wednesday when asked about the latest documents. "But that is up to the investigators.

"Any comment beyond what we placed in front of the courts is inappropriate. There are a number of criminal prosecutions that have yet to take place.

"Our job is to put it before the courts. We've done that job and the courts have done what they have seen fit to do with it."

Mr. Ford's lawyer Dennis Morris emphasized that the incidents being discussed in the court documents are in the past.

"The mayor is changing his life," Mr. Morris said during an interview on CP24. "All these people who were on your station talked about 'he should resign' or 'he change his way [sic]' just remember all this stuff happened way back in April. This isn't something that happened last week.

"As you know he's involved in support with professionals and he's at the gym every day for two hours. Take a look at him. You'll see what a tremendous change that's occurred in the last month."

City councillors continued to condemn the mayor, who has been stripped of most of his key powers, some expressing dismay at the lies and self-inflicted damage, while others professing they are well past the point of being shocked.

"I think it's pretty clear by now that Rob Ford is his own walking disaster zone," Councillor John Parker said.

Councillor Denzil Minnan-Wong, a former ally who weeks ago publicly called on the mayor to resign, said the mayor needs to give "complete disclosure" of his involvement with drugs and gang members.

The councillor raised concern about "what the implications are when the mayor of the city may be compromised by one of the worst gangs in the city."

Budget Chief Frank Di Giorgio said he thought the mayor is "going to have to deal with this" but he expected him to continue holding on. "I still think that the mayor will take the position that he wants to put it all behind him," he said. "If they aren't chargeable offences I don't think it will make a whole lot of difference."

Alleged Ford deal: Car for drug video; Court documents; Toronto mayor facing another barrage of claims

THU DEC 5 2013
By: Adrian Humphreys

Toronto Mayor Rob Ford may have offered $5,000 and a car to two men trying to sell a video of him smoking what appears to be crack cocaine seven weeks before the video was revealed in the media, according to newly revealed portions of a police document.

Toronto police were in the midst of a large drugs and guns probe targeting an alleged street gang when secretly recorded conversations led investigators to believe Mr. Ford may have not only known an incriminating video of him existed, but also tried to buy it.

New allegations from a large police investigation also claim:

- One of the men suspected of peddling the "crack video" of Mr. Ford said he also had pictures of the mayor "doing the hezza," which is a slang term for heroin;
- Alleged gang members said they were not afraid of the mayor turning them in to police because they had pictures of him "on the pipe";
- The mayor's close friend and occasional driver, Alexander Lisi, used purported influence over police as leverage in dealing with a gang, saying if he didn't get his way "the mayor would put heat on Dixon," which was the gang's territory;
- The mayor's cellphone was stolen while he was at a crack house after late-night calls were made arranging a drug delivery "because Rob Ford wants some drugs";
- Lisi exchanged marijuana to an alleged gang member for the return of Mr. Ford's stolen phone;
- Mr. Ford appears to have been set up by drug dealers who filmed him consuming drugs knowing it could be valuable, raising the spectre of blackmail;
- A man involved with alleged drug dealers said they "love and respect Rob Ford," but also "have Rob Ford on a lot of f—ked up situations," so the mayor's friends should be careful.

The newly released portions of a sworn police affidavit filed in court are the clearest explanation yet of how Mr. Ford became entwined in an explosive and elaborate police probe that eventually led to him being stripped of most of his powers by city council.

It offers key missing pieces of the puzzle of why police pored over the minutiae of Mr. Ford's life when he was never charged.

The impunity felt by alleged drug traffickers and potential blackmail might explain why police took the allegations so seriously and highlight how Mr. Ford's personal proclivities could impact his political role and made the mayor's office vulnerable.

The allegations are contained in newly revealed portions of an immense summary of a police investigation of Mr. Ford and Lisi contained within a sworn affidavit, called an Information to Obtain, filed by the police in connection with the investigation; the accuracy of the sworn affidavit has not been tested in court.

The summaries of wiretap evidence the Crown unsuccessfully fought to keep private after a legal challenge from the media, including the *National Post*, was previously blacked out when the Information to Obtain was revealed Oct. 31. The *Post* has not independently verified the police claims.

The new allegations are surprising and important—even after Mr. Ford's outlandish antics made headlines around the world and pushed him into pop-culture notoriety through late-night comedy routines and Internet memes over his crack use, "drunken stupors" and lewd commentary.

The mayor could not immediately be reached for comment.

Police investigating alleged members of the Dixon City Bloods, a Toronto gang, received court authorization to secretly monitor phones of 59 "principal known persons." The name of the mayor started popping up regularly in the probe, codenamed Project Traveller, the police document says, although never his voice.

In one conversation on March 27, conducted mostly in Somali, two men noted their "friend" was on television again, a reference to the mayor, police say; the men spoke of Mr. Ford being kicked out of an event for being drunk and the chat took place the day the *Toronto Star* reported Mr. Ford looked intoxicated at the Garrison Ball charity event.

The conversation then segued into an apparent offer to get the Ford video, according to the document.

"Remember that day he said that in front of me," said Mohamed Siad, 27, who was later identified as one of the men trying to sell the video.

"Ya, he said, 'I'll give you 5,000 and a car.' What the f—k is that?" replied Siyadin Abdi, 22, according to a sworn police affidavit filed in court. (It is possible an offer, if real, may have come through an intermediary rather than the mayor.) Mr. Siad then said he planned to meet the mayor and ask for "150," believed to mean $150,000.

Mr. Abdi said the video could also be sold to the *Star* or Gawker, a U.S. website, two media outlets later shown the video during furtive sales pitches. But Mr. Siad said he preferred going to Mr. Ford personally instead of the media; Mr. Abdi said dealing directly with the mayor was unwise and dangerous, the document says.

The police note a call was made to the mayor's office from Mr. Abdi's cellphone March 18 at 10:16 p.m. There was no answer.

When police later asked Mr. Abdi about that call, he was unco-operative and said he could not explain it, the document says.

A police analysis of the conversation concludes the men were believed to be talking about "receiving an offer from Mr. Ford in exchange for a video."

Project Traveller's wiretaps were shut down June 13, the day of police raids and 44 arrests, but the large number of calls meant a police backlog in translating and analyzing them. It was not until Aug. 28 a Somali-speaking officer translated the March 28 call, police say.

The police affidavit also reveals a remarkable series of calls allegedly involving the mayor, drugs, his friend and alleged gang members.

On April 19, at 8:14 p.m., Lisi called Mr. Ford and they spoke for 11 seconds, the document says. That was their last phone contact that night.

The document alleges later that night they were together at 15 Windsor Road, a crack house, near the Dixon Road epicentre of the Bloods' territory, likely arriving after midnight.

At 12:52 a.m., April 20, a call was placed from Liban Siyad's cellphone to the home line at 15 Windsor Road. The woman who answered, believed by police to be Elena Basso, said Mr. Ford was at the house and Mr. Siyad should come over quickly, according to a summary of evidence compiled by police. The call lasted one minute, 16 seconds.

Ms. Basso, who is also known by the nickname "Princess," has a criminal history involving prostitution and drugs. Police had monitored numerous drug calls from the house, they said.

Two minutes later, a call from Abdullahi Harun's phone also reached Mr. Siyad, instructing him to go to "Princess's" house "because Rob Ford wants some drugs," the document says. Mr. Siyad said he had already been told.

At 12:59 a.m., there was a two-minute, five-second call between two men in which one said he was "going to deal with Rob Ford right now," according to police.

At 2:18 a.m., during a one-minute, 18-second call to Mr. Siyad, Mr. Harun said he "had Rob Ford smoking on the 'dugga,'" the document says. He added he also had "so much pictures of Rob Ford doing the hezza," a slang term for heroin. Mr. Siyad said they would be valuable.

Still going at 5:51 a.m., Mr. Siyad made another call informing an unknown person the "mayor of the city, Rob Ford, was smoking his rocks today" and he would post a picture of it on Instagram, a photo-sharing website.

Mr. Ford realized his phone was missing that morning. It was a personal cellphone, registered through the Ford family's business, Deco Label. Soon, his friend Lisi was trying to get it back, police allege.

In the space of 45 minutes, Lisi called Mr. Ford's cellphone 19 times, apparently hoping whoever had it would answer, police say.

At 11:37 a.m., Lisi called Mr. Siyad. Lisi went by the nickname "Dro."

Lisi told Mr. Siyad he was "one of the guys at Elena's house last night," according to police. He then accused Mr. Siyad and his friends of stealing the mayor's phone.

"Rob is freaking out because he needs his phone," Lisi told Mr. Siyad, according to police. Mr. Siyad said he would look into it. If the mayor did not get it back, Lisi allegedly threatened, "the mayor would put heat on Dixon."

Over the next two hours, Lisi called Mr. Siyad several times about the phone. At 12:55 p.m., he said he wanted a meeting right away.

At 1:01 p.m., Mr. Siyad called an unknown man who goes by the nickname "Juice Man." The two spoke about what they would say when returning the phone to explain why they had it. (Other calls directly between Lisi and Juice Man show they knew each other.)

But then another man took Juice Man's phone, the document says. This man, an apparent superior in the group, told Mr. Siyad to make it clear when handing back the phone it was not being returned because of the threat from Lisi about getting the cops to put heat on Dixon.

"They were not pleased with the threats and indicated that they have a picture of Ford 'on the pipe,' (believed to be a crack pipe), and therefore will not tolerate his threats," the police affidavit says.

The man then offered a threat of his own, saying they "love and respect Rob Ford but they have Rob Ford on a lot of f—ked-up situations and they don't wanna say anything."

At 1:22 p.m., Lisi again called Mr. Siyad, police say. Mr. Siyad said he had the phone, but wanted to meet close by because it was cold outside. They agreed to meet at a nearby Country Style coffee shop.

Lisi said he would give him "spliffs," a slang term for marijuana, in return, the document alleges.

On Oct. 1, Lisi was charged with trafficking in marijuana, possession of proceeds of crime, possession of marijuana and conspiracy to commit an indictable offence.

On Oct. 31, the day Toronto Police Chief Bill Blair announced police had recovered a video of the mayor apparently smoking drugs, Lisi was further charged with extortion for alleged attempts to retrieve a digital video.

A timeline of events allegedly surrounding Rob Ford's lost phone

THU DEC 5 2013
By: Jake Edmiston

Toronto Mayor Rob Ford told his staff he lost his cell-phone at a public park clean-up this spring, former spokesman George Christopoulos recalled in a police interview. As Mr. Christopoulos remembered it, the mayor said he probably left it on the hood of his car and it must have slid off. It wasn't password protected, so there was major concern.

But wiretaps collected during a major guns and gangs probe outline an entirely different set of circumstances, investigators claim in recently unsealed portions of the Information to Obtain a search warrant (ITO).

The network of phone calls captured by police detail

a frenzied attempt by Mr. Ford's friend Alexander Lisi to get the phone back after a Friday night visit to what police considered a known Etobicoke crack house. None of the allegations contained in the newly released wire-tap summaries have been proven in court. As a court lifted a publication ban on the wiretaps Wednesday, the *National Post* breaks down the night the mayor lost his phone, April 20, 2013.

APRIL 20

12:52 A.M. Shortly after midnight, Liban Siyad calls 15 Windsor Road—the residence where the so-called crack video is believed to have been recorded. A female voice, suspected by investigators to be Elena Basso, answers. She says Siyad should come over quickly; Mayor Rob Ford is at her house.

12:54 A.M. Abdullahi Harun tells Siyad to go to 15 Windsor Road to deliver drugs to the mayor, according to a police summary of the intercepted phone call. Siyad says he has already spoken to Ms. Basso—who goes by "Princess."

12:59 A.M. Siyad calls "KK," which police suspect is an alias used by Abdirahaman Mohamed. KK is going "to deal with Rob Ford right now," according a police summary of the call.

2:18 A.M. More than an hour after calling to arrange the meeting, Siyad speaks again with Harun. Harun says Mr. Ford was smoking on the "dugga" and claims to have photos of the mayor "doing the hezza."

4:23 A.M. The mayor's friend and occasional driver, Alexander "Sandro" Lisi, calls Mr. Ford 19 times in under 45 minutes, according to phone records obtained by police. In court documents, investigators speculate that Lisi was constantly calling in an effort to reach the person who had the mayor's phone.

5:51 A.M. Siyad tells an unidentified caller that the mayor of Toronto was "smoking his rocks" at 15 Windsor Road, according to summaries of the wiretap. He tells the caller that he plans to put a photo of the event on Instagram.

11:37 A.M. Just before noon, the mayor's friend Alexander "Sandro" Lisi—also believed to go by "Dro"—calls Siyad and accuses him and his friend of stealing the mayor's phone when they were together at 15 Windsor Road. Lisi says the mayor is "freaking out" over the missing phone, and threatens that Mr. Ford will "put heat on" the Dixon Road complex where Siyad and his associates are believed to be based. Siyad promises to get the phone back.

1:01 P.M. Siyad calls someone only identified in police documents as Juice Man. The two discuss their excuse for having the mayor's phone. They settle on saying a friend took it accidentally. Another man takes the phone from Juice Man and instructs Siyad to make it clear that they're not returning the phone because of Lisi's threats. Siyad responds that he doesn't like being threatened and he has a photo of the mayor smoking a pipe. The unidentified man reiterates that they "love and respect" the mayor, but "they have Rob Ford in a lot of f—ked up situations."

1:22 P.M. Siyad tells Lisi he has the mayor's phone. The two arrange a meeting at a Country Style coffee shop. Lisi says he will bring Siyad "some spliffs"—common slang for marijuana cigarettes.

5:31 P.M. Siyad tells Said Duale that the mayor's driver, Mr. Lisi, gave him "1.5 of kush"—an apparent reference to a quantity of marijuana.